Six Stone Jars

God's Remedy for Fear, Worry and Anxiety

DAN MANNINGHAM

Six Stone Jars

by Dan Manningham

Scripture references are quoted from
The English Standard Version of the Bible
and where noted,
The King James Version
and The New King James Version

Cover design by Melanie Schmidt
Cover photograph by Gay Ayers
(www.gayayers.com)
Used by permission

ISBN 1-885904-75-4

PRINTED IN THE UNITED STATES OF AMERICA
BY
FOCUS PUBLISHING
Bemidji, Minnesota

Six Stone Jars

God's Remedy for Fear, Worry and Anxiety

DAN MANNINGHAM

Dedication

To Fran
wife and wise counselor
for 50 years

and

To "Beans and Greens"
and "Grape Jelly"
(you know who you are)

Table of Contents

Introduction

"Jesus promised the disciples three things—
that they would be completely fearless,
absurdly happy and in constant trouble."
-G.K. Chesterton

**Yet man is born to trouble as surely
as sparks fly upward.
Job 5:7**

Imagine this scene. You have driven a long distance and neglected to watch your fuel gauge because you have been distracted by the heavy traffic and the noisy children in the back seat. Suddenly the engine stops and you are forced to coast off the road and wait for help. You are out of gas. It is embarrassing and frustrating, but the tank is empty and you are far from any source of more.

Just at that moment a car stops behind you to ask if they can help. Seeing that you are out of gas the drivers tells you that he doesn't have any gasoline but he does have a couple of jugs of water. He suggests that you pour that water into your gas tank and see what God will do with it. So considering that you are out of options you do just that and then find that the car starts and runs as if you had poured gasoline into the gas tank.

Clearly it is not reasonable to expect that God will contradict His rules of natural order to turn water into gasoline even though we know that He can. There are other Godly rules of consequences, trials, and instruction that normally override the simple needs and desires of the moment.

But suppose that Jesus, Himself, suggested that you fill the tank with water. Would you then be surprised to find the car running normally? And what if, in a moment of fear and anxiety,

Jesus suggested that you fill six stone jars with water and wait for His blessing, would you do that?

> "A man must have an eye to God if he is to
> be enlightened by a miracle."
> -H.P.Liddon

One constant in life is trouble. People disappoint us. Relationships collapse. Careers are sidetracked. Hopes fade. Health fails. Accidents and violence happen.

Further, trouble comes with an evil twin. Trouble's twin is the mental and spiritual baggage that we call worry or anxiety or fear. Trouble happens and worry follows. Everyone knows it and no one likes it because it is painful. Fernando Ortega, singing about sleepless nights, says,

> "In those early hours I'm falling again into the river of my worries..."

When trouble strikes you can be confident that worry and anxiety will follow closely and you risk falling into it like falling into a cold, turbulent river.

In a sense, worry and anxiety are a profound and misguided form of meditation. We hold the dilemma in our mind and examine it from every angle, and consider every possible consequence. We look for all of the hurts and bruises that are likely to come from this present problem and think and think and think about them. This fear, worry and anxiety drain our reservoirs of peace, hope, joy, faith, trust and spiritual confidence, and we need something to refill those jars lest we die from thirst.

Trouble comes and worry follows and we look for help. We look for some quick relief because the pain is—well, painful.

Worry and anxiety become like acid burning away at our core and consuming our attention and our energy. They are a consequence of trouble, but they are often worse than the trouble itself.

Some look for relief in alcohol or drugs, some in sex, many in endless talk, a few in wise counsel and prayer. We long for relief from that arthritis of worry and we hope that this night at least we will not "fall into the river" because the river is bitter and rough and unrelenting. And then we awake and start meditating again and looking for some help—any help—to end the pain.

But just as God created the trouble and the worry, He had a plan from the beginning for us to cope with it. This was a comprehensive plan for us to find relief from the pain through the promises of "Living Water", the Word of Scripture, and additionally through prayer, through deliberate control of our thoughts, and through the Holy Spirit who dwells in every believer in Jesus Christ.

This is not a plan to anesthetize us and bring some form of euphoric relief. It is not a mantra that guarantees emotional comfort. It is a plan that allows us to replenish our spiritual and emotional reservoirs with the truths and promises that He has created, that He has demonstrated and that He has guaranteed. We do this with the same faith exercised by the steward at the wedding at Cana. We take the only substance available and fill our jars of peace, hope, joy, faith and trust, and spiritual confidence with prayer and memories of God's past blessings, thoughts of His great promises, perseverance, patience and praise. You do not have to spend your days meditating on the hurt and trouble of life and you do not have to fall into the dark river of worry at night. God has a remedy.

In the following chapters you will see God's plan for the spiritual warfare of combating fear and worry. These chapters will equip you to fight well but you will have to fight. You will have to pick up the equipment, learn how to use it and then recognize that God is there with you encouraging and strengthening you for each offensive stroke, each thrust and every step.

**Put on the full armor of God so that you can take your stand against the devil's schemes.
Ephesians 6:11**

I have compared these six ingredients of prayer, past blessings, promises, perseverance, patience and praise to the water Jesus commanded to be emptied into those six stone jars at the marriage in Cana. The steward of that wedding was on the brink of humiliation as the wine ran out and the guests stayed. He had run out of himself. He had run out of options. He was in serious trouble.

He was so desperate that he was willing to follow the illogical instructions of a poor carpenter who happened to be a guest. The steward was helpless to change his dilemma and because he felt hopeless he was willing to try anything.

Jesus commanded that six stone jars be filled with water. It was a simple command but without any apparent hope for the flustered steward who, nevertheless, obeyed this calm figure of spiritual authority. The jars were filled and they were filled with the only material available. Water. Plain water.

Six stone jars were filled with water and when it was tasted, it was found to be not water at all but the finest wine. This frantic steward had followed the instructions of God's Son, in faith, and found that the common substance he put into the jars was transformed into the material he desired. All it took was six stone jars, some water and a heart of obedience. But be careful to notice this: between the water and the wine was Jesus.

And not only is Jesus between the water and the wine, He is between each one of us and a righteous God.

For there is one God and one mediator between God and men, the man Christ Jesus, who gave himself as a ransom for all men (1 Timothy 2:5-6).

If you have not humbled yourself to admit your sinful nature, your actual sinful behavior, and your complete dependence on Jesus' sacrifice for that sin, you have no mediator. Without that, there is no eternal connection between you and God and there is no Jesus between the water and the wine as you read this book. It is a sobering fact of God's plan. You cannot expect God to respond to you if you have not responded to Him in the only way that He recognizes.

Whoever believes in him is not condemned, but whoever does not believe stands condemned already because he has not believed in the name of God's one and only Son (John 3:18).

But for those who have submitted to the Lordship of Jesus Christ, the following illustration of six stone jars is a simple picture of Jesus' instructions for those who live with empty jars while longing for a good measure of the wine of peace, hope, joy, faith and trust and spiritual confidence. It is intended to put flesh on God's promise that, *"you (those who have yielded to God's authority through Christ's sacrifice) did not receive a spirit that makes you a slave again to fear, but you received the Spirit of sonship. And by him we cry, 'Abba, Father.' The Spirit himself testifies with our spirit that we are God's children"* (Romans 8:15-16).

I don't expect Jesus to meet me on the highway with jars of water for my empty gas tank. I plan to keep an eye on the fuel gauge even when there are distractions. But I do know that He has given me spiritual water with which to fill my empty jars in times of fear, worry and anxiety.

Six stone jars. Six empty vessels that God suggests we fill with the powerful, cleansing, refreshing and life sustaining water of His Word and the resources that Word describes. You could think of those spiritual resources as the water He has provided for us to fill those six stone jars that have been drained by the pressures and distractions of life. And the substance of that spiritual water with which to fill our empty jars is in six parts: prayer, past blessings, promises, perseverance, patience and praise

And then He changes that water to wine. And between, always between them, is Jesus. He is God's remedy for fear, worry and anxiety.

> "We can only appreciate the miracle of a
> sunrise if we have waited in the darkness"
> -Anonymous

> **Though you have made me see troubles,**
> **many and bitter, you will restore my life again;**
> **from the depths of the earth you will again**
> **bring me up. You will increase my honor**
> **and comfort me once again.**
> **Psalm 71:20-21**

Chapter One

The Certainty of Trouble and His Evil Twin Worry

"Trouble is the common denominator of
living. It is the great equalizer."
-Soren Kierkegaard

"Nobody, as long as he moves about
among the chaotic currents of life,
is without trouble."
-Carl Gustav Jung

**Beloved, do not be surprised at the fiery trial
when it comes upon you to test you, as though
something strange were happening to you.
1 Peter 4:12**

There is a spirit abroad in the world that assumes that peace and happiness are the natural state of man. If you listen to television commercials or daily talk shows, or most of what passes for general conversation, you would be likely to assume that man was destined to live a life of general well being, occasionally interrupted by temporary difficulties. This common worldview assumes that trouble is an aberration and that when it occurs it is a disruption of the normal state of things. Life, they say, is meant to be good and trouble is the exception.

The biblical worldview could not be more different. While God created man to live in a paradise of pleasure, that plan ended with Adam and Eve's sin of disobedience. God spoke immediatel after that first sin to inform our first parents that, *"I will greatly increase your pains in childbearing; with pain you will give birth to children,"* and *"Cursed is the ground because of you;*

through painful toil you will eat of it all the days of your life... By the sweat of your brow you will eat your food until you return to the ground" (Genesis 3:16-19).

"Trouble makes us one with every
human being in the world."
-Oliver Wendell Holmes

Since man's fall in the Garden of Eden it has been his natural, God-given fate to live a life replete with trouble. Our many difficulties, struggles and problems are not some exception from a norm of peace and tranquility. Troubles are the very essence of the human experience and they are precisely in accord with God's plan for this world and for our individual lives. Trouble is normal, ordinary and common to all. Jesus, Himself, said so.

"The world – it is a wilderness where
tears are hung on every tree."
-Thomas Hood

In this world you will have trouble.
But take heart! I have overcome the world.
John 16:33

Trouble is the natural state of life on earth and it comes in two shapes: Temptations and Trials.

TEMPTATIONS arise from the evil desires of our hearts which are then illuminated and encouraged by Satan. They do not originate with God although He does permit them. They do not originate with Satan although he exhorts them and enhances them to harm us and separate us from God. Temptations originate in the fallen heart of you and me and they are a serious component of the trouble that stalks us every day of this life.

When tempted, no one should say, "God is tempting
me." For God cannot be tempted by evil, nor does

he tempt anyone; ¹⁴but each one is tempted when, by his own evil desire, he is dragged away and enticed. ¹⁵Then, after desire has conceived, it gives birth to sin; and sin, when it is full-grown, gives birth to death (James 1:13-15).

Resisting temptation is strenuous work. It requires vigilance and effort and determination, energized and empowered by the indwelling Holy Spirit. God has given us limitless resources to resist temptation but he has given us the responsibility to use those resources faithfully. There is no temptation that is unique. There is no temptation that you cannot resist. God has made a way to escape them all but it requires work and dedication. And although you cannot do it alone, you can do it by the power of the Holy Spirit who dwells within every believer in Christ. You can do it out of love for the Savior who shed His blood to purchase us from the marketplace of sin and adopt us into God's family.

> "No degree of temptation justifies
> any degree of sin."
> -Nathaniel Parker Willis

No temptation has seized you except what is common to man. And God is faithful; he will not let you be tempted beyond what you can bear. But when you are tempted, he will also provide a way out so that you can stand up under it.
1 Corinthians 10:13

TRIALS are the other flavor of trouble. Trials are situations designed by God to draw us closer to Him. Job was tried as no other man in Scripture and his trial was specifically authorized by God even though God Himself described Job as *"blameless and upright, a man who fears God and shuns evil"* (Job 1:1).

As a result of his trial, Job's understanding of God was magnified and God's blessings on Job were multiplied. It was a truly horrible trial but it drew Job closer to his Redeemer in a way that made all other things insignificant.

Joseph was tried by the cruelty of his brothers and the dishonesty of his employer's wife. There is not a single criticism of Joseph in the Bible and yet he was tried in difficult and painful ways that brought him closer and deeper in his relationship with God. In the end, Joseph was able to say to his brothers who were afraid of retribution, *"Fear not: for am I in the place of God? And as for you, you meant evil against me; but God meant it for good"* (Genesis 50:19-20).

Daniel was severely tried, even to the ultimate experience of rooming with hungry lions for an evening. God tried Daniel for reasons we will never know, but that trial strengthened and matured Daniel in ways that no other experience could.

Someone has said it this way, "God is always up to something good." Even in trouble, God is up to refining us and strengthening our character if we will let Him. *"We also rejoice in our sufferings, because we know that suffering produces perseverance; perseverance, character; and character, hope"* (Romans 5:3-4).

One form of trial is the transgressions of other people in our lives. Inconsiderate supervisors at work, spiteful neighbors at home, malicious family members and others will sin against us and cause deep painful hurt.

> "Troubles are the tools by which God
> fashions us for better things."
> -Henry Ward Beecher

Trials are one of God's tools to draw us closer. They are customary and normal in this life and we can be certain of that because Jesus Himself told us so. We get sick, we suffer terrible accidents, we lose friends, we are betrayed, we are unfairly criticized, we experience financial crises, we are lonely, we are cheated, we are abandoned, we are insulted, and we are snubbed. The catalogue of trouble is vast and it is a part of every human life.

When I go on the internet and GOOGLE "Trouble," I get 292 million responses. "Sorrow" gets 36 million. "Pain" 342 million. "Lonely" 104 million. Temptations and trials are an integral part of this life of flesh. God said so...

> "Into each life some rain must fall. Some
> days must be dark and dreary."
> -Longfellow

> **Man that is born of woman is of
> few days and full of trouble.
> Job 14:1**

None of this is surprising to God. He told us dozens of times in Scripture to "fear not", "don't be anxious", and "be free from cares". He told us those things precisely because He knew that our lives would suffer considerable trouble. Jesus promised (promised!) that *"in this world you will have trouble"*. He could say that because He often shapes the trouble for our good. Just read the book of Job over again and see. God sometimes shapes and fashions trouble for us in order to create people of character and perseverance.

> "Suffering is the fertile soil into which God
> transplants every growing Christian."
> -Anonymous

Oswald Chambers reminds us that the basis of human life is tragedy; that we are built with a bigger capacity for pain than for joy, that the undertone of all life is sorrow. And that the great expression and revelation of God in the world is the revelation of the cross, not of joy.

It was never God's plan for us to have these troubles, but when Eve ate the fruit and Adam followed, their virus of sin spread through the entire race. And one consequence of sin is trouble. No one is immune.

Trouble has an evil twin named "Worry," also known as "Fear" or "Anxiety". This twin goes by several aliases: apprehension, angst, fretfulness, anguish, concern and more. He is the traveling companion of trouble and he has multiple identities.

Our troubles, trials and temptations are inevitably accompanied by this thuggish twin who takes great delight in abusing and torturing us. In many cases worry inflicts more actual damage than the trouble itself. Worry is a pernicious, nasty, malignant enemy that saps our strength, distracts our thinking and weakens our faith. It is as common as trouble but there is a distinction. *Trouble comes from the outside and worry comes from the heart.* We cannot avoid all of our troubles but we can do something about the worry it incites.

> "Worry is a thin stream of fear trickling
> through the mind. If encouraged, it cuts a
> channel into which all thoughts are drained."
> -Arthur Somers Roche

And we know that we can do something about our worries because God has relentlessly instructed us to *"fear not"*, *"be anxious for nothing"*, *"do not worry"*, and *"be not dismayed"*. Clearly He would not have repeated these imperatives over and over if He had not left us some means of complying.

And there is more. God has promised us great joy in the assurance of His love and care, and in our eternal destiny to be with Him forever. He has promised us great joy and has given us tools to find that joy.

> **For his anger lasts only a moment, but his favor lasts a lifetime; weeping may remain for a night, but rejoicing comes in the morning (Psalm 30:5).**

> **Those who sow in tears will reap with songs of joy. He who goes out weeping, carrying seed to sow, will return with songs of joy, carrying sheaves with him (Psalm 126:5-6).**

All through the Bible is a theme of hope. Hope for tomorrow. Hope for the future. Hope for eternity. All that hope is based on the sure and firm hand of a loving Father God who is so beautifully represented as the Prodigal's father watching the road for his son to come home. He is a Father of absolute holiness and perfection; a Father of justice; a Father who cannot tolerate sin, but a Father who responds immediately and personally to our confession and repentance.

> "Behind the cloud the starlight lurks, Through showers the sunbeam falls; For God, who loveth all His works, Has left His hope for all."
> -John Greenleaf Whittier

So the question is not whether we can *"fear not"* or *"be anxious for nothing"*, the question is how? In the midst of trials and temptations, what resources has God given me for the spiritual battle? What are the weapons God has given us to use in the battle?

> "All the water in the world cannot sink a ship— unless the water starts getting inside. All the troubles in the world can't sink a human being—unless those troubles invade his inner life."
> -Vera Werblo

In the following chapters you will see six specific resources to use in this spiritual fight against fear, worry and anxiety. I have compared them to the water used to fill those six stone jars mentioned in the second chapter of the gospel of John. If you are willing to use these resources you will find considerable victory over fear, worry and anxiety. You will not find deliverance in the form of some spiritual valium. You will not find some liturgical magic that will stop the emotions, but you will find tools that are sharp and available and useful in your battle with fear, worry and anxiety.

You will have trouble. You will suffer trials and temptations and they will be accompanied by that hooligan named "Worry". But in the midst of trouble and worry God has crafted wonderful and powerful tools for us to resist fear. There are many ways to look at those tools, but in this book you will see them through the lens of the miracle of six stone jars.

"Well, poor Christian, how much do you
think there is of God—of His Spirit, of
His Word—in your fears?

"Why, just none at all, for it cannot be that
such fears are the workings of the Spirit of
God. These are not His doings. Do you not
see the very paw of the devil in them? For
these fears tend to harden your heart."
-John Bunyan (paraphrased)

**For God did not give us a spirit of fear, but a
spirit of power, of love and of self-discipline.
2 Timothy 1:7**

Chapter Two

The Miracle of Six Stone Jars

"Difficulty is the very atmosphere of miracle; it is miracle in its first stage. If it is to be a great miracle, the condition is not difficulty, but impossibility."
-S.D. Gordon

Men of Israel, listen to this: Jesus of Nazareth was a man accredited by God to you by miracles, wonders and signs, which God did among you through him, as you yourselves know.
Acts 2:22

Jesus' first public miracle happened very early; shortly after His 40-day fast and temptation in the deserts of Judea. Forty days in which He endured the heat and the fleas, the stony ground and the copper sky. Forty days in which His body weakened but His spirit became so strengthened by its pure communion with the Father that Jesus was able to resist the direct and personal temptation of that great liar, Satan. And not only resist, but actually drive away the great deceiver with his tail between his legs. It is amazing what faith and spiritual discipline can do!

It happened shortly after He chose His first disciples; Andrew, Peter, Philip and Nathanael: two fishermen, one cynic and one country boy who was slow to grasp Jesus' authority and power.

He was 30 years old and He had just just laid down his hammers and saws and chisels to begin His great ministry as Messiah and Savior. He had only recently transitioned from building furniture to building men, a far more noble and ambitious goal.

This miracle happened at a wedding and it happened reluctantly and it is the very first reported miracle of Jesus' ministry.

> On the third day a wedding took place at Cana in Galilee. Jesus' mother was there, and Jesus and his disciples had also been invited to the wedding. When the wine was gone, Jesus' mother said to him, "They have no more wine."
>
> "Dear woman, why do you involve me?" Jesus replied. "My time has not yet come." His mother said to the servants, "Do whatever he tells you."
>
> Nearby stood six stone water jars, the kind used by the Jews for ceremonial washing, each holding from twenty to thirty gallons. Jesus said to the servants, "Fill the jars with water"; so they filled them to the brim. Then he told them, "Now draw some out and take it to the master of the banquet."
>
> They did so, and the master of the banquet tasted the water that had been turned into wine (John 2:1-9).

Jewish weddings were elaborate affairs. The actual ceremony took place in the evening after a time of feasting. The bride and her father would meander through the dusty streets of the town so that everyone would have a chance to congratulate her. When they arrived at the groom's house the ceremony would take place and then there would be days of celebration in which the bride and groom were fêted. During this week, the groom's family was expected to provide food and drink in abundance.

Nearby stood six stone water jars, the kind used by the Jews for ceremonial washing, each holding from twenty to thirty gallons.

Religious law required the guests to wash their hands and feet before participating in the feast because Jews became ceremonially unclean simply through the normal processes of the day. This washing was not a matter of personal hygiene but of Jewish ceremonial cleanliness. They didn't really know or care about germs, but they did care about appearing to be clean in God's eyes, as though God could only see their skin.

In order to allow this ceremonial washing, the host of this wedding had prepared six stone jars full of water. You could walk in, dip some water, wash up and look good for God.

The host had also supplied a store of wine but—much to his surprise—not enough. Some think that the arrival of Jesus and His friends tipped the balance but it is just as likely that the guests were thirstier than anyone had expected. It gets hot in Judea. There were a lot of dates and raisins, lamb and pita bread to wash down. People eat and drink more when they are enjoying the company of friends and family. There are many explanations but in any event the wine ran out.

That was not just an inconvenience, it was a shameful humiliation. Imagine inviting special guests for Thanksgiving dinner and finding that you didn't prepare enough turkey and you will get some idea of this social embarrassment. Imagine Easter with a miniature ham. Not having sufficient wine was inconceivable. It just couldn't happen. You had to have enough wine for everyone at a Jewish wedding and that was the steward's responsibility.

When the wine was gone, Jesus' mother said to him, "They have no more wine."

It was so much like a woman to hear the whispered comments of the waiters as they became increasingly aware that the wine would run out. There is a lovely feminine dimension to this sensitivity. It is a sweet mystery when women detect by their curious intuition that something is wrong and that someone needs help. It is the wonderful integration of two brain hemispheres that is so uniquely female. Something in Mary could just sense that there was a problem and at the very same moment of awareness she could divine a solution.

His mother said to the servants, "Do whatever he tells you."

It was also a natural thing for a Mom to do. She had watched her son for 30 years and certainly knew His divine nature, His caring heart and helping hands. Perhaps she had seen Him helping the needy in Nazareth, the kids with damaged toys and the widows with broken front doors. We can assume that her suggestion at this wedding is fully consistent with her suggestions at home over the past many years when Jesus' skill as a carpenter was used in several ways to help friends and neighbors. She knew His ability. She knew His compassionate heart.

She also knew His divine origin. She knew that her son would *"be great and will be called the Son of the Most High. The Lord God will give him the throne of his father David, and he will reign over the house of Jacob forever; his kingdom will never end"* (Luke 1:23-33) because the angel had told her before His birth. She knew of what he was capable and she added the motherly element of compassion for the helpless.

This motherly element caused her to suggest that Jesus perform one more act of kindness for the discomfited steward who would bear all the criticism for this failure. It was as natural as pointing Jesus to a neighbor with a broken loom or an old man who needed a new walking stick.

Think of it like this: these simple five words of Mary to the wine stewards are a hazy but pleasant insight into those years of

Jesus' life about which the Gospels are silent. We have no details of Jesus' life between his visit to the temple at age 13 and the beginning of His public ministry 17 years later. We know that he worked as a carpenter and we assume that He lived at home, but the rest is lost to history. Mary's five words are a small knot hole into those years as she confidently suggests that they *"do whatever He tells you."*

Surely this suggestion comes from years of observing a compassionate and capable son who long ago grew into manhood and household leadership and who apparently was capable of amazing and miraculous things. Only a mother who knew her son would suggest such a thing. Only a mother with great confidence in her son's divine nature and compassionate spirit would suggest that He would find a way when there was no way. It is a sweet and powerful testimony to what Jesus had been doing for years in private.

> **"Dear woman, why do you involve me?" Jesus replied. "My time has not yet come."**

Jesus' response to His mother seems out of character. Why would this perfect son talk so abruptly? Isn't He already deeply involved with His mother; so what has changed?

Actually, this phrase "why do you involve me" was common in the Hebrew culture, and not as rude as it might sound in another language. It is intended to put distance between the two parties. You can read similar rebukes in several parts of the Old Testament (Judges 11:12; 2 Samuel 16:10) and they are always used in the sense of, "It would be best if you don't get involved. This is between me and someone else. Let me handle it."

It appears that Jesus is describing a change of relationship with His beloved mother. He has begun His public ministry and it was time for Mary to adjust her thinking to see Him as the promised Messiah and not her special boy. It is a moment that all mothers and sons must come to in order to have a healthy relationship beyond childhood. It is not disrespectful; it is a simple statement regarding their changed circumstances. He is now about His Father's business full time but *"the time has not yet come."* His death and resurrection and glorification are all in the future and there is serious work to be done in the meantime. His time of sacrifice had not yet come although He was willing to begin the work here with a simple miracle.

He would resolve the wine crisis, but they could not know that this was only the beginning.

Jesus said to the servants, "Fill the jars with water"; so they filled them to the brim.

He commanded the jars to be filled with water; the old, stale water of ceremonialism. This was the water that could wash your hands but not your heart. It was the water of ritual without righteousness. It was just water; the most common material on the planet that Jesus himself had created.

"Fill the jars with water?" What good could that do? It makes us wonder how the Jews or anyone else ever thought that ceremonial details could bring them into an intimate relationship with a perfect and Holy God.

It is also interesting that he includes the servants in His plan. Jesus could have filled the jars Himself but He instructed the stewards to do so. In the same way, He could fill our churches and orphanages and soup kitchens but He asks us to do that. He knows that we will never really be a part of His family if we are not willing to be involved. It was always His plan that we fill the jars and He will turn them into something good and useful. It's a nice touch. It has never changed. We pour the water. He makes the wine. And always, Jesus is in the middle.

Then he told them, "Now draw some out and take it to the master of the banquet." They did so, and the master of the banquet tasted the water that had been turned into wine.

So the servants filled those six stone jars with water and Jesus transformed that liquid into the finest wine. The guests at the wedding exclaimed to the bridegroom, *"Everyone serves the good wine first, and when people have drunk freely, then the poor wine. But you have kept the good wine until now"* (John 2:10). In a sweet act of symbolism He replaced the water of a legal code with the wine of grace. He transformed the stagnant water of ceremony into a delicious wine of mercy and grace and forgiveness with the power to cleanse hearts. It hadn't all been explained at this point but when we look back through the lens of God's New Testament we can see the symbolism.

But don't miss this point that is the purpose of this book: This miracle was also a rich symbol of how the Savior enters into the difficult moments of our lives, even in mundane things, and how he enriches those moments. He doesn't ask much of us; just the faith to fill jars with water.

"Prayer is the frame of the bridge from weeping
to doing, built across the canyon of despair."
-James Gilliom

**Do not be anxious about anything, but in everything, by prayer and petition, with thanksgiving, present your requests to God.
Philippians 4:6**

The first jar we will fill with prayer; just the simple act of presenting our requests directly to Him. He wants to hear from us. It is not a fruitless effort. God has promised that our prayers are heard; that they smell to Him like sweet incense; that if we ask He will answer.

In every crisis there is an empty jar waiting to be filled with our prayers as the steward filled a jar with water. It may seem to be a futile and unnatural effort, but since God has commanded the procedure we can just fill the jar and wait for His wine.

> "Shut out all your past except that which will
> help you weather your tomorrows."
> -William Osler

> **When a lion or a bear came and carried off a sheep
> from the flock, I went after it, struck it and rescued the
> sheep from its mouth. When it turned on me, I seized
> it by its hair, struck it and killed it. Your servant has
> killed both the lion and the bear; this uncircumcised
> Philistine will be like one of them.
> 1 Samuel 17:34-36**

The second jar should be filled with a celebration of God's mercies and gifts in your past. God has filled our lives with His blessings. We have enjoyed food and shelter and relationships and friends and eternal salvation itself. The words above (1 Samuel 17:34-36) were spoken by David as he volunteered to slay the giant, Goliath. He was boasting only in the fact that he knew God would save him from that Philistine. We have experienced miracles if we will just see them. In fact we *are* walking miracles if we are believers in Christ and therefore children of God. The list of past blessings is normally obscured by the immediate troubles we face but they are there in multitudes. God has blessed us abundantly and will bless us again. He has enabled us to kill lions and bears and He will strengthen us against the present Goliath.

> "Faith in the promises makes the future present,
> and the heirship possession. It is thus 'the
> substance of things hoped for.'"
> -John Gill

24

**He who dwells in the shelter of the Most High
will rest in the shadow of the Almighty. I will
say of the LORD, "He is my refuge and my
fortress, my God, in whom I trust."
Psalm 91:1-2**

Next, fill the third jar with a deliberate remembrance of the promises He has made throughout Scripture. There are many. He promised to be our Shepherd, our Refuge, our Fortress our Shield, our Defender. He promised to hear our prayers, every one. He promised to love us, protect us, and uphold us with His righteous right arm. Start your own list. But buy a large notebook because as you start digging into Scripture you will discover the list of God's promises is very large.

"Brave admiral, say but one good word:
What shall we do when hope is gone?"
The words leapt like a leaping sword:
"Sail on! Sail on! Sail on and on!"
-Joaquin Miller, Columbus

**Therefore, since we are surrounded by such a great
cloud of witnesses, let us throw off everything that
hinders and the sin that so easily entangles, and let us
run with perseverance the race marked out for us.
Hebrews 12:1-3**

The fourth jar is the most difficult to fill. It is our steady perseverance in the midst of trials. In this we have the great example of Job; wavering, anxious, unsettled, discouraged but persevering to the point of saying, *"Even if He kills me I will hope in Him."*

Oswald Chambers paraphrased that verse like this, *"Though He slay me, I will trust in the fact that He is full of the integrity I believe Him to be, and I will wait for Him"* (Job 13:15).

We are called to persevere in sickness and financial stress and loneliness simply because we trust that God is with us. It is encouraging to know that perseverance has a purpose which is to create maturity in us as we children of God grow up: *"Perseverance must finish its work so that you may be mature and complete, not lacking anything"* (James 1:4).

"Patience is the ballast of the soul, that will keep it
from rolling and tumbling in the greatest storms."
-Charles Hopkins

**But the fruit of the Spirit is love, joy, peace, patience...
Galatians 5:22**

The fifth jar must be filled with the water of patience. Patience: that most challenging of human measures precisely because it requires no action, no achievement, no difficult planning or list-making nor anything else.

Patience is that difficult feat of waiting, trusting, hoping. It is actually a mostly futile pursuit for those who do not know a personal and loving God. But for those who have deliberately and completely submitted their lives to the authority of the God who sent His own Son to die for our sins ... to those there is great value in patience.

The platform for that patience is our simple trust that He is always at work for good. He is the great physician applying the perfect medication for the desired results. He is the Good Shepherd who knows more than the sheep and who is worth following because He has promised that He is leading us to green pastures and still waters. He is our heavenly "Abba" Father, always acting in our best interests.

Theodore Beza was John Calvin's successor in the protestant struggle for existence in reformation Europe. His adult life was spent in defending and instructing the reformation church, often against the civil powers of France.

When Theodore Beza defended that church to the King of Navarre he said, "Sire, it belongs to God's church rather to suffer blows than to strike them; but let it be your pleasure to remember that the church is an anvil which hath worn out many a hammer."

Lord, help us to be an anvil. Help us to wear out the hammers of our lives. In times of stress let us fill our jars with the water of patience.

> "The climax of God's happiness is the delight
> He takes in the echoes of His excellence in
> the praises of His people".
> -John Piper

> **Praise the LORD, O my soul; all my inmost**
> **being, praise his holy name. Praise the LORD,**
> **O my soul, and forget not all his benefits.**
> **Psalm 103:1-2**

The last jar should be topped off with praise to God who loves us and constantly prepares the best for us. David's exhortation to praise in Psalm 103 was based on his recommendation that *"we forget not His benefits."* Good advice. When we remember His benefits (remember jar number three?) we have solid ground on which to praise Him.

In the midst of trials and temptations it is not easy to sing praise. It is not the first thing that comes to mind. It is a sacrifice for a troubled and anxious heart to pause for praise to God. I think it is, in fact, exactly what the writer of the book of Hebrews had in mind when he said, *"Through Jesus, therefore, let us continually offer to God a sacrifice of praise"* (Hebrews 13:15).

Six stone jars filled with water. The radical change that occurred inside those original stone jars is a sweet sign of how Jesus offers to transform the water of our prayers and perseverance and praise into the wine of assurance and comfort. When we fill those jars with obedience and faith He changes the ordinary trouble of life into something rich and valuable. He changes shortage into wisdom. He changes our simple offerings of water into the wine of peace and joy because He is in the middle of it all.

"Miracles are intended to assist those who are already seeking God. They are not intended to inflict a sense of God's power and presence and truth upon those who do not wish to know more about Him."
-H.P. Liddon

Jesus said to them, "I did one miracle, and you are all astonished."
John 7:21

Chapter Three

The Prayer Jar

"Next to the wonder of seeing my Savior will
be, I think, the wonder that I made so little
use of the power of prayer."
-D.L. Moody

**The prayer of a righteous man is
powerful and effective.
James 5:16b**

The most obvious stone jar the Lord has given us to fill is the prayer jar. It stands there in the busy clutter of our Christian life waiting to be filled with the water of prayer so that God can turn that water into the wine of His perfect guidance and wisdom for our life.

We are the stewards at this feast. We come to Him with empty jars: with faded hopes and broken dreams and grinding anxieties. He has a simple plan which requires nothing but faith from us: fill the jar with prayer and he will turn it into wine. It may not always be the wine we imagine or expect or want but always His best wine.

Do not be anxious about anything, but in everything, by prayer and petition, with thanksgiving, present your requests to God. And the peace of God, which transcends all understanding, will guard your hearts and your minds in Christ Jesus (Philippians 4:6-7).

In 1999 my wife, Fran and I spent six months in West Africa where I volunteered as a pilot with a mission aviation organization after spending 38 years flying professionally. As we prepared for this trip our local church was very encouraging and supportive and one of our Pastor's young daughters was particularly concerned for our safety. In her 11-year-old understanding of Africa and its potential dangers, she was afraid that we might be attacked by lions or tigers or some other predatory cat. So she prayed faithfully that "Dan and Fran would be safe from African cats." She was a sweet girl with a sweet prayer.

Actually, West Africa has very few predatory cats and so Kristen's prayer would seem to have been unnecessary to anyone knowledgeable about the local hazards. Kristen was not an expert on African wildlife but she was anxious for the safety of older friends so she filled that jar of concern with the water she had on hand. She filled it with a simple request for safety and waited on God. Kristen filled her prayer jar and waited for God to convert her water to wine.

Our time in Africa was rich and enjoyable and without a single sighting of wild cats. The flying was challenging and agreeable for a life-long pilot and we flew an interesting mix of flights including direct service to missionaries, medical evacuation of anyone who called and some commercial service to supplement the high cost of operating a complex, turbine powered airplane in humanitarian service.

One of our commercial contracts was with a large gold mining firm which operated an extensive facility in the Sahel wilderness. Nearly 1500 people lived and worked there in a spot remote from any connection to the rest of civilization except by satellite link or airplane and some large trucks that trundled across a couple hundred miles of open desert to bring bulky cargo and diesel fuel. It was a remote and isolated compound and our flights were often the only practical means to carry mail or other critical items.

On one such flight I was asked by the wife of one of the residents if I would carry her cat back to the capital city for treatment by a veterinarian. Someone would meet the airplane and take the cat that was caged in a very solid cardboard box with tiny air holes. It was a simple favor I was happy to do.

We strapped the cat box securely on top of some cargo behind our ten passengers and prepared to leave. As we started the engines, the whine from the turbines apparently frightened the cat and she began caterwauling with such volume that we could hear her clearly in the cockpit over the engine noises. The cat was obviously distressed, but there was nothing to do but complete the short flight and assume she would recover from the psychological trauma. Everyone knows that cats are tough.

As we started the takeoff roll the tortured shrieking became even louder. It was painful to hear the animal in such distress but we were on the way home and that would take less than an hour. Our little airplane climbed quickly into the brilliant African sunshine until at about 13,000 feet the cat suddenly appeared in the cockpit. She was not mad, or aggravated or annoyed. No, this cat was quite simply berserk. Her teeth were bared, her ears flat, her eyes like slits and her claws fully out. Her first action was to bite the copilot on the hand opening a wound that looked like he had been sliced to the bone with a scalpel. There was a lot of blood. It was an ugly wound.

She then streaked to the back of the airplane before returning to the cockpit. And that began a cycle of racing from front to back and at each visit to the cockpit trying again to bite and claw us with particular interest in our eyes. In short order the copilot was incapacitated with pain and we were both scratched and bloody and thoroughly distracted from our flight duties as we attempted to defend ourselves from a demon cat that was intent on ripping our eyes out. The cockpit looked and felt like a war zone.

At some point I was able to trap the cat against the windshield with our clipboard and a brave passenger came forward to take control of the poor animal. All of this high drama took place in a very short time, perhaps a minute or less, but when I recovered from the immediate threat I found that the cat had tripped the autopilot switch and the airplane was banked at 90 degrees and on its way to being upside down. It was also beginning to enter a steep dive and would soon have exceeded its maximum allowable speed. We had arrested the berserk cat with little time to spare and, as it turned out, were able to right the airplane with no damage. We had been delivered "safe from African cats."

"Keep praying, but be thankful that God's
answers are wiser than your prayers."
-William Culbertson

**Be joyful in hope, patient in affliction, faithful in prayer.
Romans 12:12**

Kristen had been faithful in prayer. She had filled her prayer jar with water and waited for the wine. In the end, the wine was different than what she may have imagined but it was wine, pure and good.

It is an easy thing to let that prayer jar stand empty. We struggle with worry and anxiety and fear for our families, our health, our friends and in some perverse fashion allow that fear, worry and anxiety to distract us from the simple act of prayer, of filling that first jar. We meditate on our problems, examining them on every level and for every possible outcome and forget to fill the prayer jar. We are often unfaithful stewards, just ignoring the advice of the Savior and leaving our jars empty. It is all too common and altogether tragic.

"Why pray when you can worry?"
-Anonymous

Scripture is filled with instructions to pray and with encouragement that God hears and answers our prayers.

- **The prayer of a righteous man is powerful and effective (James 5:16).**
- **He will respond to the prayer of the destitute; He will not despise their plea (Psalm 102:17).**
- **For the eyes of the Lord are on the righteous and his ears are attentive to their prayer (1 Peter 3:12).**

There are numerous examples in Scripture of God's answer to prayer. There are dozens of times when His people came to the end of their selves and began to fill that empty jar with the water of prayer.

- When Israel was dying of thirst in the desert, Moses prayed and God told him to throw a tree into the undrinkable water they were near. A tree, mind you! Water into the prayer jar. Tree into the mud. Wine in the form of drinkable water for all of Israel (Exodus 15).
- Elijah was threatened by 850 pagan priests. He had no way out. He was forced to trust God, so he prayed for fire to consume his sacrifice in a divine act of fireworks as a testimony to God's greatness. Elijah filled the jar with the water of his prayer and God poured out fire that licked up everything there, the sacrifice, the wood, the stones and the water they had poured over it.
- Hannah watched her biological clock tic away and longed for a son. Her husband's other wife had children, but not Hannah. At one point she prayed so fervently that her husband thought she was drunk but she was just busy filling the prayer jar with the water of her requests to God. And God turned that water into the wine of a son

1 Samuel 1:13 states Eli, the High Priest, thought she was drunk (not her husband).

named Samuel who would become one of the greatest of all prophets.

There are countless examples of answered prayer although they are not all answered exactly as the one who prayed would have wanted. I suspect that our greatest barrier to prayer is the fear that God will not give us precisely what we pray for even though He never promised that. He did promise to turn our water of prayer into His gift of wine but He has always reserved the authority to determine what that wine would be like. In fact, it is precisely why He also encouraged us to:

Trust in the LORD with all your heart and lean not on your own understanding; in all your ways acknowledge him, and he will direct your paths (Proverbs 3:5, 6).

This was important for the wine steward at the wedding in Cana and it is important for us as we pray in obedience to God's teaching on prayer. We are simply the fillers of the jar. The water we use for that filling is the desire of our heart for the immediate circumstances of our lives. Are you sick, discouraged, broke, lonely, tempted, and anxious? Fill the prayer jar with the water of your request and trust that your Father God hears and considers and responds with the perfect wine of His choosing. *"Our God is in heaven; he does whatever pleases him"* (Psalm 115:3).

It is impossible to disconnect prayer from trust in God and His wisdom. But mind you, we do not trust in a promise to grant our every wish. We trust in His wisdom to answer as a Father who is always interested in our welfare. We do not pray for candy and expect our Father to deliver. We pray for His direct involvement in the complexities of our lives to work out the details for His glory and our holiness and this He promises to do.

- **Commit your way to the LORD; trust in him and he will do this: He will make your righteousness shine like the dawn, the justice of your cause like the noonday sun (Psalm 37:5-6).**
- **You will keep in perfect peace him whose mind is steadfast, because he trusts in you (Isaiah 26:3).**

Just consider Jesus, the Son of God, and our Savior. If anyone knew and appreciated the value of prayer it was Him. There are several gospel accounts of Jesus withdrawing from His friends and followers and retreating into the solitude of prayer. There is no record of the prayers themselves, but it is reasonable to assume that Jesus prayed for many of the things we pray for.

In Matthew 6 he went up a mountain to pray. In Luke 6 it records an all night prayer session. Clearly Jesus understood the value of bringing His cares and concerns and thanks directly to His heavenly Father, and He understood that because of His unshakable faith and trust in the Father's wisdom and goodness.

Without that faith and trust our prayers are weak and shabby. When you fill the prayer jar, do so with the confidence that God knows and hears your heart desires. And that He sifts all of that together in order to formulate an answer that is perfectly suited to your circumstances in eternity.

Incidentally, it is interesting to note that Jesus' private prayers were often lengthy, even all night. But His public prayers are short. Is there a message there for us?

But notice that even the Son of God did not always receive the answer he desired. As He approached the final days of His life, knowing that those days would culminate in His death on a cruel cross, He was *"a man of sorrows and acquainted with grief"*. It was not even the physical pain that was so intimidating. It was the idea of being separated from His Father and covered with the filth of sin from all mankind. Someone has said, "There was no sin in Him but God put sin on Him". Jesus, Himself said, *"My soul is overwhelmed with sorrow to the point of death."* This was tough beyond our imagination.

> "Spread out your petitions before God, and then say, 'Thy will, not mine, be done.' The sweetest lesson I have learned in God's school is to let the Lord choose for me."
> -Dwight L. Moody

So Jesus came to the Garden of Gethsemane after having his last meal with His friends and He came with a heart of sorrow and grief. He knew that circumstances were moving rapidly toward His sacrificial death. He was out of options. There was no clever plan available to avoid the brutal end. So in His *"sorrow to the point of death"* He filled the prayer jar with this simple request, *"My Father, if it is possible, may this cup be taken from me."* That was it. That was all that was necessary to fill that jar because it was accompanied with total faith and trust in the Father.

Now be sure to notice this: His Father did turn that prayer into wine but not the wine Jesus had prayed for. He turned it into the wine of suffering and death that opened the doors of heaven for millions of sinners who would believe. God the Father had weighed all of the details in the balance, including the emotional prayer of His Son. And weighing all of that the Father concluded that He *"so loved the World that He would give His one and only Son."* And Jesus was not spared "the cup" of suffering but we reap the blessing of His imputed righteousness.

Water into wine. But not always the wine we might choose. And then, sometimes it is and more. And always it is by God's perfect wisdom.

"More things are wrought by prayer
than this world dreams of."
-Tennyson

On September 9, 1943, following the defeat of the Axis powers in North Africa and Sicily, the Allies launched a major invasion of mainland Italy at the southern town of Salerno. The amphibious assault was launched against powerful German forces under the most difficult of circumstances.

That evening, Rees Howells, the founder of the Bible College of Wales, announced to his students at their evening prayer meeting, "The Lord has burdened me with the invasion of Salerno. I believe our men are in great difficulties and the Lord has told me that unless we pray through, they are in danger of losing their hold."

And so they prayed. They joined together filling that stone jar and they prayed until it was filled to the brim. At 11:00 that night they broke into spontaneous singing and rejoicing because there was a mysterious but powerful sense among them that God had wrought a miracle on the bloody beachhead at Salerno.

At midnight they gathered around the radio to hear the latest news from that front. The news was sobering. The radio reporter said that unless some miracle happened the invasion would fail and the Allies would be pushed back into the sea. Thousands of lives were at stake as well as the future conduct of the war.

The next morning the newspaper headline read, "MIRACLE AT SALERNO". The account, written by a reporter who was on the scene described it approximately like this, "I was with our advanced troops in the invasion of Salerno. The enemy artillery was advancing rapidly and with ceaseless firing. The noise was terrible and it was obvious that unless a miracle happened our troops could never hold up the advance long enough for the beachhead to be established.

"Suddenly, for no accountable reason, the firing ceased and the Nazi artillery stopped its advance. A deathly stillness settled on the scene. We waited in breathless anticipation, but nothing happened. I looked at my watch – it was eleven o'clock at night. "Still we waited, but nothing happened; and nothing happened all night, but those hours made all the difference to the invasion. By the morning the beachhead was established."

Truly there was a miracle at Salerno. At 11:00 pm on September 9, 1943, God turned the water of students' prayers into the sweet wine of protection for thousands of Allied troops.

If you read the accounts of the battle for Salerno you will find that the succeeding days involved fierce fighting with the outcome never sure. Three days later the German 10th Army launched a counterattack that lasted three days and almost succeeded. The fighting was some of the fiercest of the war, but ten days after the invasion the Allied forces were established and within a month, the whole of southern Italy was in Allied hands.

"Who can know the mind of God?" But who can deny that on the night of September 9, 1943 water was turned to wine. And Jesus was in the middle.

"What a friend we have in Jesus,
All our sins and griefs to bear!
What a privilege to carry
Everything to God in prayer!
O what peace we often forfeit,
O what needless pail we bear,
All because we do not carry
Everything to God in prayer."
-Joseph Medlicott Scriven

**Do not be anxious about anything, but in
everything, by prayer and petition, with
thanksgiving, present your requests to God.
Philippians 4:6**

When Kristen was anxious about her older friends she prayed that they would "be safe from African cats" and Jesus turned that water into the wine of comfort in their safety from a very unexpected cat.

When Jesus prayed in the Garden of Gethsemane that His Father would remove the crushing culpability for the sins of all mankind, the Father listened and considered –as He does with each and every prayer – and determined that His plan was better than the immediate request of His Son. How difficult that must have been: water turned into bitter but eternally profitable wine.

When the students at the Bible College of Wales prayed for safety for the soldiers and sailors invading the beaches of Salerno, God answered with a startling miracle. Wine from water.

In each case someone thought and determined to fill that empty jar with the water of prayer, and then just wait for God's wine. In each case they prayed with the faith to trust God's judgment for the outcome.

Water into wine, but always with Jesus in between.

It is important to remember always that prayer is the cause and effect of our relationship with God through His Son. Prayer was never meant to be in a formula of scripted words that are empowered in some poetic manner. Prayer is the conscious connection between you and the God who loves you. Prayer is a conversation in which you empty your heart to God and He promises to listen and answer with His infinite wisdom. He is your Father. You are His beloved child. He wants to hear from you but not by formula. Tell Him your heart. Ask for His answers. Jesus promised His Father's compassion and care.

> **Which of you fathers, if your son asks for a fish, will give him a snake instead? Or if he asks for an egg, will give him a scorpion? If you then, though you are evil, know how to give good gifts to your children, how much more will your Father in heaven give the Holy Spirit to those who ask him (Luke 11:11-13).**

Sometimes it is difficult to pray. Sometimes our emotions control our prayers and in those times it is helpful to use psalms and Bible prayers to allow our knowledge of God to lead our emotions.

And finally there is this: God has even made provision for those times when we are simply too distraught, too tired, and too distracted to pray. He has promised that, *"In the same way, the Spirit helps us in our weakness. We do not know what we ought to pray for, but the Spirit himself intercedes for us with groans that words cannot express"* (Romans 8:26).

Even when we are too tired to fill our own jars, the Holy Spirit will do that for us if we but ask.

> "Come ye disconsolate, where'er ye languish
> Come to the mercy seat, fervently kneel. Here
> bring your wounded hearts, here tell your anguish:
> Earth has no sorrow that heaven cannot heal."
> -Thomas Moore

> **Ask and it will be given to you; seek and you will find; knock and the door will be opened to you. [10]For everyone who asks receives; he who seeks finds; and to him who knocks, the door will be opened.**
> **Luke 11:9**

Chapter Four

The Jar of Past Blessings

"God gave us memories so that we
could have roses in December."
-Francis Bacon

**Praise the LORD, O my soul, and
forget not all his benefits.
Psalm 103:2**

We come now to the second jar. I can imagine the steward at
the wedding at Cana directing his workers to bring the water up
from the well and fill the stone jars one at a time It must have
been strenuous work to fill a jar that held 30 gallons of water. It
certainly required dedication and effort to fill six of them. I can
imagine a bucket brigade between the well and the jars. This was
180 gallons of water, three 55 gallon drums in modern measure.

Remember this: Jesus did not miraculously fill those big
jars. He directed the steward to do so and left the decision and
that work to him. When they had been filled, Jesus did perform
the miracle of transformation, but only after the steward had
accepted His directive and done his part. This was not a quick
or easy job and neither is fighting the spiritual war against fear,
worry and anxiety. In our analogy here there are six jars to fill.
This is not some formula for manipulating God, but it is a mental
picture of the tools that God has given us to wage war against
our dominating concerns and apprehensions.

"Miracles are intended to assist those who are
already seeking God. They are not intended to inflict
a sense of God's power and presence and truth upon
those who do not wish to know more about Him."
-H.P. Liddon

This second jar is designed to hold our memories of past blessings. In order to fill this jar we will have to scour our memory for those times when God has reached into our lives with divine favor. Actually, it is a concept that God Himself initiated. He created the Passover feast so that Israel would remember their deliverance from the angel of death. When Israel crossed the Jordan River into the Promised Land, God commanded a stone marker to be built so that they would never forget His care for 40 years in the wilderness. Jesus created the ordinance of communion so that we would always remember His sacrifice for us. God created the rainbow so that we would remember His covenant after the flood.

In order to fill this jar with memories of personal blessings we must dig through the historical data in our brains to find those times when God has answered prayer in visible ways; comforted our hearts, healed our bodies, protected our children, provided for our needs, delivered us from danger and more. There are many of those in every life but memory is a strange and difficult thing.

> "Memory is the cabinet of imagination, the treasury of reason, the registry of conscience and the council chamber of thought."
> -Saint Basil

It is common in recent years to compare our memory to the electronic workings of a computer. Scientists have even attempted to measure the volume of human memory in terms that are related to digital processing. Some have calculated that the human memory can retain 10^{20} bits of information, many times the capability of even a supercomputer.

But the problem with human memory is that it is distorted by our sinful nature and thus cannot function with the simple predictability of a computer. Human memory is naturally driven by human nature, and so we are prone to fix on memories that are worldly, sensual and selfish, or simply allow our minds to wander without control.

One testimony to this human trait is the instinct to build monuments and statues and parks and elegant buildings as a means of not forgetting men and events. Everywhere in the world these markers have been erected for the sole purpose of remembering a single person or occasion. It is clear that without some deliberate effort our memories lose the blessings of the past and focus on the troubles of the present. It is also clear that we tend to focus our memories on the things of human history rather than the blessings of divine favor.

Our job here is to deliberately filter our memories so as to fill a jar with remembrances of God's blessings.

> "For my remembrance recalls me, and pleasant
> is it to me, O Lord, to confess to Thee"
> -Augustine

One thing I do know. I was blind but now I see!
John 9:25b

If we are to fill a jar with memories of God's blessings it certainly should begin with memories of our own salvation. As we drive to church in nice clothes and a polished mini-van and perfect children it is important for us to remember that without Christ we were *"wretched, pitiful, poor, blind and naked"*. We are sinners, saved by grace.

Paul reminded the Ephesians that before their repentance they were *"separate from Christ ... and foreigners to the covenants of the promise, without hope and without God in the world. But now in Christ Jesus you who once were far away have been brought near through the blood of Christ"* (Ephesians 2:12).

What memory could be more meaningful and encouraging than to consider that the God of the universe has reached down to redeem a wretched sinner? And by the way, it is good to have a clear understanding of that word we translate "redeem" because it is rich with meaning.

English translations of the New Testament use our word "redeem" for two different Greek words. They each have a similar meaning of "ransomed" or "purchased" but the word that brings a vivid scene to mind is the Greek "exagorazo" which literally means to purchase and remove from the market; to buy something and take it home.

If you have been to a third world market place you know that it is a large open space with countless little stalls where vegetables and meat, trinkets and simple household items and clothing are displayed on ramshackle tables. It is noisy and smelly and dusty with a great bustle of people all shopping at the same time. If you buy something from one of those stalls and take it home you have "redeemed" it. But notice that, not only have you made it your personal property, you have denied it to anyone who comes after you. You have purchased it and removed it from further availability in the market place. It is gone. Off the shelf.

"Oh! Sorry! I just sold that one. It's gone."

Now imagine another stall in that market place where slaves are sold. "Honey, let's look at slaves in the market. Our old one is wearing out." So, you find the slave stall and decide on a particular one, agree on a price after some haggling, pay the slave master and "redeem" your new slave. He is bought and paid for and removed from the market. He is yours and you take him home.

"Oh! Sorry! I just sold that one. It's gone"

Now remember that we who have placed our eternal faith in Jesus Christ were once slaves. We were slaves to sinful desires and passions when Jesus Christ purchased us and removed us from that market. And we had a price.

"How much is this one?"

"Oh, that fellow is expensive."

"Well, how much? $1000? $10,000? $1 Million?"

"No. Only blood will do. And only the blood of God's Son. That's the price. Nothing else. Take it or leave it."

So the price was paid on Calvary and we have been "redeemed". And now we are the slaves of righteousness and—get this—not just slaves but adopted sons and daughters of the Living God. What a blessing! What a memory.

> "To live is to remember and to remember is to live."
> -Samuel Butler

I love the story of David as a teen, taking bread and grain to his brothers who were encamped with the army of Israel in the Valley of Elah where they confronted the Philistines, Israel's mortal enemy. He was just a kid. Think of the teen who delivers your newspaper or the high school student behind the counter when you order hamburgers.

David delivered the food and was shocked to see the mighty warriors of Israel so intimidated by those pagans across the valley. Israel's God had sworn His love and protection on the nation. He repeatedly told them He would be their strength and their fortress. David was indignant that those pagans should be allowed to continue mocking Yahweh's chosen people and that they would put up with it. *"Who is this uncircumcised Philistine that he should defy the armies of the living God?"* (1 Samuel 17:26b).

Exactly, David! Who was this guy who was mocking the very God of the universe and His hand-picked people? Did this guy know who he was dealing with?

So David said to the King and his generals, "Let me take a shot at him."

Saul, in response says, "David, you're out of your league. You are a boy and he is a fighting giant with military skills he has been honing since before he was your age. You're volunteering for a suicide mission."

Your servant has killed both the lion and the bear; this uncircumcised Philistine will be like one of them (1 Samuel 17:34).

I like to imagine David at this moment. He is looking at the most powerful fighting machine anyone has ever seen. Goliath is nine feet tall. He is covered with 125 pounds of heavy armor and carrying multiple weapons including a spear with a 15 pound warhead that he knows how to use. He is big and smelly and hairy. He is a scary guy for even the biggest man in Israel. In fact, Saul *was* the biggest man in Israel and he was afraid of Goliath.

Surely David himself could see that this was a poor match; actually no match at all. David was smaller, younger, and far less experienced. He had no hope whatsoever of overpowering Goliath or defeating him with sword play. Really, David's entire proposal was preposterous except for one thing: God had promised and He was able.

In that moment David knew that God was able because he remembered that he had killed a lion and a bear with his bare hands, and he knew that those feats had been accomplished solely by the power of God working through him. David wasn't up to killing wild beasts with his bare hands. No one does that to a lion or a bear but David remembered doing it and knew it was the power of God that had enabled him.

David remembered the lion and the bear and that remembrance gave him the confidence that all of Israel lacked.

You, too, have killed lions and bears by the power of God. You have memories of impossible situations where you experienced the power of God to do what you, alone, could not. You have seen the miracle of stony hearts turned into flesh, of physical protection in impossible circumstances, of comfort when there was no comfort, of personal gifts and talents that could only have come from a loving God.

Remember your lions and bears. There are more of them than you think because our memories are so unreliable. Search for them in your memory and pour them into this jar.

> "Like a bird singing in the rain, let grateful
> memories survive in time of trouble."
> -Robert Louis Stevenson

**I remember the days of long ago; I meditate
on all your works and consider
what your hands have done.
Psalm 143:5**

Every believer has countless past blessings, large and small, for which to be thankful. Our problem is that we do not default to the "thankful" position but are more prone to mumble in our spirit, "What have you done for me lately?"

Think of an adopted child you may know who came from an orphanage somewhere in Brazil or Russia or anywhere. This child had been rejected or discarded in some way and was relegated to an institution that would feed and shelter it but little else. Suddenly a married couple appears on the scene and spends considerable time and money to bring this orphan into their loving home where he discovers warmth and affection and security. We hope that orphan will never forget the blessings associated with his adoption.

Well, we were orphans. We were adopted into God's family. We were removed from the uncaring institution of this world and brought into God's family where we have countless brothers and sisters.

Think about a person you know who is a cancer survivor. They will certainly have vivid memories of that day when a somber doctor explained their disease and its threat to their life and well being. They will remember the nauseating treatments and the terrible fatigue and pain of the treatments and finally the joyful pronouncement that they are cancer free.

You have been healed from lots of things. If not cancer, then injuries and common colds and the flu, toothaches and pulled muscles, migraines and poison ivy. Further, there are multiple diseases that you have not contracted that have debilitated others: malaria, cholera, yellow fever, dysentery. What blessings God has given in the area of health.

Think of your home. It may not be much but it beats a dumpster in New York or a refugee camp in Sudan.

Think of that automobile accident you did not have or the one you survived.

Think of the time your child was missing in the mall and then found safe.

Think of friends who have helped, of family members who have challenged you, of someone who has influenced your life for good, of some stranger who helped in an emergency.

Think of the birth of healthy children.

Think of that storm that did not devastate you home and some holiday when the family was well.

Look around your home at the pictures and mementoes and keepsakes that are designed to remind you of pleasant events and then remember the blessings that are associated with each one.

"Unless we remember we cannot understand"
–Edward M. Forster

**I will remember the deeds of the LORD; yes,
I will remember your miracles of long ago.
Psalm 77:11**

Remembering our past blessings is a way of recalling and understanding the mercy and favor of God. We don't strive to remember for simple gratification. We search our memory for past blessings to remind us of God's wisdom, authority, mercy and goodness. And out of that we derive confidence in the midst of fear and worry and anxiety. Remembering past blessings is not a new idea:

- God told Israel to remember that He had delivered them from bondage in Israel.
- God told Israel to remember how He had provided land for each one of the twelve tribes.
- The Jews established the holiday of Purim to remember their salvation under Queen Esther.

- In a psalm of praise David commands his people to, *"Remember the wonders (God) has done, his miracles, and the judgments he pronounced."* Remember.
- Jesus told his disciples to remember the miracle of loaves and fishes.

This jar requires some diligent work to fill. We do not naturally savor all of the kindnesses of the past. We are ungrateful children who casually accept gifts and blessings from God and then move on with our lives. We are much more prone to focus on the difficulties of the present and worry that nothing can be done, that God is deaf, that prayer is hollow.

Read about the experiences of the children of Israel as Moses, under the direction of God, led them out of their bondage to the Egyptians. They wandered (and grumbled) for 40 years before they came to the Promised Land of Canaan. On the eve of this great blessing Moses admonished the people to look back and remember all that God had done for them (Deuteronomy 11). Not only to remember, but to teach their children and write the blessings on the doorpost of their houses.

Remember that honoring God's commands brings blessings. Not only did God part the Red Sea for them to leave Egypt, but at the end of their journey, they crossed the Jordan River on dry land. When they had all crossed over, God instructed Joshua to take up 12 stones from the middle of the riverbed to build a memorial on the other side.

> **He said to the sons of Israel, "When your children ask their father in time to come, saying, 'What are these stones?', then you shall inform your children, saying, 'Israel crossed this Jordan on dry ground. For the Lord your God dried up the waters of the Jordan before you until you had crossed, just as the Lord your God had done to**

the Red Sea, which He dried up before us until we had crossed; that all the peoples of the earth may know that the hand of the Lord is mighty, so that you may fear the Lord your God forever'" (Joshua 4:21-24).

In order to dip water from your past to fill this jar you will want some paper and pencil to record your thoughts because we are, by nature, forgetful and ungrateful. Make a list of God's blessings in your life and then add to it as you remember more. Keep it up until you have 30 gallons worth, pour it in and wait for Jesus.

Past blessings in; encouragement out. And always, Jesus in the middle as the miracle worker.

"Human life, old and young, takes place
between hope and remembrance."
-Franz Grillparzer.

I will meditate on all your works and
consider all your mighty deeds.
Psalm 77:12

Six Stone Jars

Chapter Five

The Promise Jar

"Faith in the promises makes the future present
and the heirship possession. It is thus
'the substance of things hoped for.'"
-John Gill

**For no matter how many promises God has made,
they are "Yes" in Christ. And so through Him the
"Amen" is spoken by us to the glory of God.
2 Corinthians 1:20**

Fill your third jar with meditation on God's promises. Now understand that meditation is not some mystical act of allowing your mind to drift where it will. That is reverie, day dreaming, or abstract musing with no clear focus.

Filling this empty jar with meditation on God's promises is the deliberate mental and spiritual work of recalling and savoring all that He has promised along with His power and willingness to follow through on those great and precious promises.

Someone has said that the Bible contains 30,000 promises. Peter called these *"very great and precious"* and so should we. We who walk by faith have built our entire hope on the promises of God for salvation, for forgiveness, for eternal life and much more. In the same way, we ought to search for God's promises for encouragement, strength, protection and peace in the midst of fear, worry and anxiety. And the very mental and spiritual act of appreciating the promises of God is our means of filling this jar with the water of His Word, by faith, and waiting with patience for the wine He creates.

"Hypocrisy can afford to be magnificent in its
promises; for never intending to go beyond
promises, it costs nothing."
-Edmund Burke

Russell Edward Herman died on October 28, 1993, in Illinois.
This exceptionally generous man left enormous sums of money
and gold to thousands of people he didn't even know:

- To the inhabitants of Gallatin County, $2.41 Billion
- To the town of Cave-In-Rock, Il $2.41 Billion
- To the city of East Saint Louis, IL $2.41 Billion
- To each of the 50 states of the union $2.41 Billion
- To the state of Illinois Health and Education Fund 1.5 Billion
- To the American people for retirement of the entire national debt $6 Trillion

Herman's generosity was unprecedented. Trillions of dollars
for personal and public welfare, but there was a catch: Herman
never did have any money. He was an eccentric who thought
he could collect on a wrinkled and aged Peruvian government
bond found in an old Bible and combine that money with some
oddball interpretation of the American national debt and tax
system to redistribute the Federal treasury.

Russell Edward Herman made enormous promises to a
lot of people. He apparently had convinced himself that these
promises were valid, but his premises were all wrong and he
was never able to fulfill anything he promised. The Peruvian
government bond was worthless. The U.S treasury was not
available for redistribution. Even assuming that his intentions
were fully honorable, he did not have the means to deliver what
he had pledged.

"Shall the promises fail? Is God unfaithful?
Is there inability or unwillingness to perform?"
-John Gill

In those questions, John Gill has raised two fundamental questions about any promise: does the one who promises have the *ability* to perform as promised? Does the one who promises have the *willingness* to perform?

Russell Edward Herman did not have the ability. He was willing but not able. The case of Tamerlane and the city of Sebastia is somewhat different.

Sebastia was the ancient name of Sivas located in modern day Turkey and currently the capitol city of Sivas Province. It is today a bustling trade center of almost 300,000 people and has been an important city since long before Christ.

In 1400 Tamerlane (Timur the Lame) besieged the city which was known then as Sebastia. Tamerlane was a Turko-Mongol tyrant and conqueror at the beginning of the 15th century. He was steeped in Persian culture and aspired to restore the Mongol Empire which had dominated Asia and much of Europe 200 years earlier. He was ruthless, cruel and merciless. He was fond of leaving mountains of human skulls outside the cities he conquered: 70,000 in Tikrit, 90,000 in Baghdad, 20,000 in Aleppo. Some think that 17 million people died in his conquests.

Tamerlane conquered all of central Asia from Western China to Turkey and from the Russian border to the Holy Land. He was an early proponent of propaganda in warfare by sending spies into unconquered lands with horrifying stories of what would happen if they resisted. When Timur besieged Sebastia with its population of 100,000 he promised that if the city surrendered he would shed no blood, a generous promise from such a brutal conqueror.

Intimidated by Tamerlane's reputation for wanton brutality, Sebastia did surrender and Tamerlane and his army did not shed even a drop of blood. They simply buried everyone in Sebastia alive. 100,000 people. No blood, but no mercy either. Unlike Russell Edward Herman, Tamerlane had the means to keep his promise but he was not willing.

"Magnificent promises are always to be suspected."
-Theodore Parker

Our lives are filled with empty promises, failed vows, broken contracts, forgotten pledges. We make and receive countless of these and our human track record of promise keeping is dismal. Marriage vows are shredded in divorce court. Loans are never repaid despite the initial pledge. Promises to call or visit or write are forgotten or avoided. The picture of human promises is not pretty.

Many promises are made by people who simply do not have the means to keep their word. Some of those are simply being deceptive and some may have every intention of fulfilling the promise but ultimately, they do not have the means.

Many more promises are made by those who are simply unwilling to be faithful. They have the means but they are unwilling to part with the money or the time or the sheer effort. It is discouraging and disturbing and many who have endured multiple failed promises simply retreat behind a cynical veneer that assumes all promises are bogus. Why even listen to a promise when I have been disappointed so many times? Children just give up on Dad taking them fishing and wives abandon any hope that the bedroom will ever be painted. Employees abandon any hope of that promised raise and customers turn to another vendor because the promises of performance were just that, only promises. And this list doesn't even start to inventory the incredible and abundant empty promises of any political campaign that are beamed to our radios and televisions incessantly during election years.

You might say that those broken promises are all understandable because of man's fallen nature, and you would be right. Despite that, legal systems in virtually all countries include firm language on the proper fulfillment of contracts, oaths, pledges, treaties and promises. Even secularists realize the value of promise-keeping to the good order of society. They can see the value and debate the merits of satisfying oaths and pledges and treaties but they lack the means and the willingness to follow through when self interest intervenes because God is not in it.

"God never made a promise that was
too good to be true."
-Dwight L. Moody

**Let us hold unswervingly to the hope we profess, for he who promised is faithful.
Hebrews 10:23**

All these experiences of failed human promises can be a hindrance to believing the promises of God. It is tempting to become cynical, skeptical, and suspicious. We may discount the very concept of promises actually being fulfilled, and the thought of filling up a jar with the promises of God seems futile. After all, what can He do? What does He know? Why would He care?

**For nothing is impossible with God.
Luke 1:37**

What can God do? He can do anything. He is God. He is not a god at war with other gods; He is The God and He can do anything. It is a theme that is foundational to all we believe and all that is written in our Bibles. God is omnipotent. Job reminded himself of that basic fact after God had spoken to Him, *"I know that you can do all things; no plan of yours can be thwarted"* (Job 42:2).

Job's profession was correct but it was late. Job suffered through all of his sorrows and finally heard the very voice of God before he acknowledged firmly and publicly, *"You can do all things."* We can avoid much fear, worry and anxiety by acknowledging and savoring that thought in our times of difficulty. God can do all things. He has promised that.

Great is our Lord and mighty in power; His understanding has no limit (Psalm 147:5).

What does He know? Well, He knows everything. He knows every sparrow that falls. Imagine that! My yard is filled with sparrows every summer. They are everywhere, especially in the bird feeders. They chatter and bicker with each other, mate and lay eggs. They hatch and fledge and fly, and when a tiny sparrow crashes into a window and falls to the ground, God sees this and He cares. Jesus said, *"Fear not, therefore; ye are of more value than many sparrows"* (Matthew 10:31).

He knows every hair on our heads. Six billion heads and approximately 100,000 hairs each amounts to, well, a lot of hairs. He knows them all. And He knows the events that are causing your fear and worry and anxiety. He knows. And He doesn't just know as an observer, He cares as a Father.

Cast all your anxiety on him because he cares for you (1 Peter 5:7).

Why would He care? We cannot fathom the answer to this question. We cannot know why a holy God would care about sinful, unfaithful people who deserve hell instead of mercy. We just know He does because He has told us (promised us) that He does.

He has promised us that He is *"the Father of compassion and the God of all comfort"* (2 Corinthians 1:3) but He does not tell us why.

Be still, and know that I am God (Psalm 46:10).

What can God do? Anything!

What does God know? Everything!

Why does God care? We don't know, but He has told us clearly that He does.

Your experience of unkept promises from other people should not undermine your confidence in God. His promises are true, faithful and sure.

He is able. He is willing.

You can fill this jar with His promises and wait in confidence for Him to make the wine. Promises in. Wine out. Jesus in the middle of it all.

> "God pays as He promises; all His payments
> are made in pure gold."
> -Thomas Brooks

**For no matter how many promises God has
made, they are "Yes" in Christ.
1 Corinthians 1:20**

It is always comforting to have solid ground to stand on, especially when we are at the edge of uncertainty. At the rim of the Grand Canyon it is good to pick your spot so that you can have confidence that you are standing on an immovable rock as you survey the scene. In the midst of fear and worry and anxiety it is equally good to find solid spiritual ground for support.

"On Christ the solid rock I stand. All other
ground is sinking sand."
-Edward Mote

**For who is God besides the LORD? And
who is the Rock except our God?
Psalm 18:31**

A news item some time ago recorded the experiences of nine coal miners who were caught in a flooded mine. The frigid water broke through into their work space and quickly filled it. As their only means of self preservation, the miners climbed up onto a rock that was the highest point in their part of the mine. Eventually the water rose to their chests and higher but stabilized there. As they stood there with just enough head room to breathe in the dark and the cold, they prayed for deliverance. Eventually a shaft was drilled to supply them with fresh air and rescuers broke through to bring them to safety. The miners had been saved by standing on a rock.

It would be interesting to know if those miners were familiar with Psalm 62 in which David professes his confidence in God, *"He alone is my rock and my salvation;... I will never be shaken."*

He is our rock. He is the same yesterday, today and tomorrow. We can stand on Him with confidence. He has promised. Put that in the jar.

"Our hearts are restless until they find rest in God."
-Augustine

**My soul finds rest in God alone.
Psalm 62:1**

There are times when we all need rest. If you have spent the day traveling or shopping or working hard there will come a moment when you simply want to sit and rest for a few moments, or more. The human system simply runs out of vigor and longs to sit or lie down and find some respite from the fatigue. It longs for a place to rest.

I know a missionary who was trying to translate this concept of resting in God into a tribal language in Brazil. He had searched for the right word for months and none of the options offered by his tribal friends captured the idea of fully and completely resting in God, of reposing on the One who holds the world in His hand.

One day a local man came back from a long and tiring hunting trip in the jungle and walked onto my friend's front porch, tired, thirsty and hungry. He stashed his bow and spears in a corner and then, because he was so tired he simply flopped onto an old couch that was there to find some rest. At that moment my friend asked him what the word for what he had just done was. What was the tribal word for just throwing oneself onto a bed because the fatigue was so great? What was the word they would use to describe a man who is so tired that he just drops everything to lie down and rest?

I don't know what that tribal word was but I know that my friend rejoiced to find that word he needed to convey the idea of our soul's rest in God to a primitive people who understood fatigue but who struggled to understand the God of Scripture.

You can find rest in God. He has promised. It is another promise that belongs in this jar.

> "Our God, our help in ages past
> Our Hope for years to come
> Our shelter from the stormy blast
> And our eternal home."
> -Isaac Watts

**God is our refuge and strength, an
ever-present help in trouble.
Psalm 46:1**

During the time when Saul was King of Israel and David had been anointed by Samuel to be the next king, there was great tension in the land. David had been anointed but Saul still had the power. It was a period of great danger for David as Saul repeatedly hunted him and tried to kill him. During much of this time, David lived in the wilderness where he sought shelter in caves.

There are times when we all feel like living in a cave. It is a human instinct to retreat from trouble and look for protective shelter. Pilots are taught to stay with their aircraft if they are brought down in the wilderness because without a refuge from the weather and from predatory animals their chances of survival diminish.

In times of crisis when we struggle with fear and worry and anxiety, it is good to know that while we may be exposed to the dangers of this world we can find refuge in the God Who loves us and has proved His love by dying for us and who waits for us in eternity. When we struggle it is good to remember that God Himself is our refuge.

"Tarry at the promise till God meets you there.
He always returns by way of His promises."
-Anonymous

**I rejoice in your promise like one
who finds great spoil.
Psalm 119:162**

If we would have the confidence to fill a jar with the promises of God in times of fear, worry, and anxiety, it would be good for us to have a mental collection of promises that He has made. There are far too many to remember but there are categories of promises that are particularly helpful when life is difficult.

God has filled His Word with His promises to us. He has promised to be

- **Our Rock:** *"For who is God besides the Lord? And who is the Rock except our God?"* (Psalm 18:32).
- **Our Rest:** *"My soul finds rest in God alone"* (Psalm 62:1).
- **Our Refuge:** *"God is our refuge and strength, an ever-present help in trouble"* (Psalm 46:1).
- **Our Rescuer:** *"Grace and peace to you from God our Father and the Lord Jesus Christ who gave himself for our sins to rescue us from the present evil age"* (Galatians 1:3).
- **Our Shepherd:** *"The Lord is my shepherd; I shall not be in want"* (Psalm 23:1).
- **Our Hope:** *"May the God of hope fill you with all joy and peace as you trust in him, so that you may overflow with hope by the power of the Holy spirit"* (Romans 15:13).
- **Our Salvation:** *"My soul finds rest in God alone; my salvation comes from him"* (Psalm 62:1).
- **Our Comforter:** *"Praise be to the God and Father of our Lord Jesus Christ, the Father of compassion and the God of all comfort"* (1 Corinthians 1:3).
- **Our Friend:** *"A man of many companions may come to ruin, but there is a friend who sticks closer than a brother"* (Proverbs 18:24).
- **He has promised to forgive us:** *"For I will forgive their wickedness and will remember their sins no more"* (Hebrews 8:12).
- **To Strengthen us, and To Support us with His Righteous Right Arm:** *"So do not fear, for I am with you; do not be dismayed, for I am your God. I will strengthen you and help you; I will uphold you with my righteous right hand"* (Isaiah 41:10).

- **To Help us:** *"Surely god is my help; the Lord is the one who sustains me"* (Psalm 54:4).

This promise jar is one of the easiest to fill because there is so much material to fill it with. You will find almost endless promises in God's Word, and if you pour them into this jar He will turn them into the wine of comfort and encouragement.

In those times of fear and worry and anxiety, spend some time searching Scripture for the abundant promises of God. Make a list. Meditate on each one. Savor them. Pour them into the jar.

Promises in; assurance out. Jesus as the agent of change.

"Standing on the promises I cannot fall,
Listening every moment to the Spirit's call,
Resting in my Savior as my all in all,
Standing on the promises of God"
-R Kelso Carter

**My eyes stay open through the watches of the night that I may meditate on your promises.
Psalm 119:148**

Chapter Six

The Perserverance Jar

"Nay, do you not see with your eyes daily, that
perseverance is a very great part of the Cross?
Why else do men so soon grow weary?"
-John Bunyan

**Therefore, since we are surrounded by such a great
cloud of witnesses, let us throw off everything that
hinders and the sin that so easily entangles, and let
us run with perseverance the race marked out for us.
Hebrews 12:1**

This may be the toughest jar of all to fill. Perseverance,
by definition, means enduring through difficulty and
disappointment for the long term. It means steady persistence
in the face of opposition and distress. It means keeping on,
keeping on, and it gets old. It just gets old.

Perseverance is very different from patience. Patience is an
expression of faith through calm endurance in which we just
"be still and know that God is God." Patience tolerates delay; it
endures without complaint, it stays still and waits for God.
Patience is passive.

Perseverance is active. Perseverance involves steadfast,
active pursuit of a goal, despite difficulties or obstacles. It
presses through the trials of life with all of the appropriate
actions. Perseverance is dynamic in that it persists in all the
right activities even when they are difficult and seem ineffective.
Perseverance is pursuing the right actions in a difficult time with
a clear focus. Perseverance may include periods of patience but
it is very different over all.

Patience is waiting for God. Perseverance is pressing on toward the Godly goal when it is uncomfortable.

This may be the toughest jar to fill because it keeps leaking out the bottom. We persevere through times of fear and worry and anxiety with the help of a merciful and powerful God—but we tire of it all. The jar leaks and needs to be replenished with, well, more perseverance. We see those missing footprints in the sand and realize that He has been carrying us and it is time to walk on our own again. It is time to persevere.

But perseverance is a highly regarded virtue in Scripture. It is a virtue that is developed and perfected through adversity and one that leads to other virtues such as "character" and "maturity" and "hope". The Biblical progression is this: suffering and trials lead to perseverance and perseverance builds character which leads to maturity and hope (Romans 5:3-5, James 1:2-4). So filling this jar is difficult and annoying and tiring, but the benefits are real and valuable.

> "To pray and not to do our best to accomplish
> that for which we pray is to insult God."
> -Sir Stafford Cripps

> **Have nothing to do with godless myths and**
> **old wives' tales; rather, train yourself to be godly. ⁸For**
> **physical training is of some value, but godliness**
> **has value for all things, holding promise**
> **for both the present life and the life to come.**
> **1 Timothy 4:7-8**

One great aid to perseverance is preparation. The people we see as great heroes of perseverance are normally those who have trained themselves well before circumstances required that difficult task of pressing on during hard times.

Some time ago I watched a former member of the Russian Army Spetsnaz, their version of Special Forces soldiers, interviewed on television. Spetsnaz troops are trained to a standard that may be unequalled in the world. They are Navy Seals and Green Berets and local SWAT teams all rolled into one highly disciplined and endlessly training fighting machine. Their skills are extraordinary and multiple and they are routinely used in the most difficult combat and civil crisis situations. Very few personnel in any military unit in the world are trained to the level of Spetsnaz soldiers and very few have as much and as varied combat experience.

During the interview this former soldier demonstrated some of his specific skills in the various martial arts, knife throwing, marksmanship with multiple weapons, explosives usage, etc. His skills were not just impressive, they were eye-watering. Then he made a most insightful comment...

This survivor of multiple combat experiences said, "People think that when you are exposed to a combat situation you will rise to the occasion. But, you don't. You don't rise to the occasion. You fall to the level of your training."

Think about that. When I am confronted with a crisis of any kind, I will not rise in some magical way to command the situation. Instead, I will fall back on the preparations I have made for such a situation.

If my dinner mate gags on a piece of meat, I will not suddenly and heroically apply the correct medical treatment unless I have prepared myself with specific training in the Heimlich maneuver. If my friend has a heart attack on the golf course, I will not rise to the occasion and gallantly restore his heartbeat unless I have been thoroughly trained in CPR.

If I encounter an emotional or spiritual crisis I will not suddenly rise to the occasion; I will fall to the level of training in Godliness that has preceded that crisis. Paul knew that when he told Timothy to *"train himself in righteousness."*

Actually the word Paul uses here is "gumnazo", the Greek word from which we derive the English word "gymnasium". Paul knew that Timothy and all of us must train our hearts with the same seriousness and intensity as an athlete trains his body.

"Train yourself, Timothy. You will not rise to the occasion. You will fall to your level of preparation."

The twelfth chapter of Hebrews lists several requirements for perseverance and none of them come naturally:

- Throw off anything that holds you back and be very careful to avoid that favorite sin that entangles you (verse 1).
- Have a clear and focused vision of Jesus, your Savior and Lord. (verse 2).
- Endure the present hardship as something that is a Godly and useful discipline (verse 7).
- Strengthen yourself. Suck it up. Trust in God who knows all about your circumstances (verse 12).
- Be at peace with those around you (verse 14).
- Be thankful and worship God (verse 28).

Elsewhere Scripture instructs us to be students of God's Word, to integrate ourselves into a community of believers, to develop a high moral standard, to cultivate a strong family, to love our spouses sacrificially. Train yourself in Godliness.

But, even when you get most of this right, it will seem like the jar is leaking. Perseverance is rough.

We love those stories of remarkable perseverance precisely because we know how difficult it is and how often we have failed. We know it is the mark of a mature Christian but we sense that our maturity is lacking. Perseverance can be done, but only to the extent that we are willing to train in Godliness and to the extent that we are willing to trust in God.

You can persevere. You can start by memorizing and practicing those principles in Hebrews 12. Or just memorize the chapter. Or train (*gumnazo*) yourself in Godliness from the whole counsel of Scripture. Or consider Job.

> "God, who foresaw your tribulation, has
> specially armed you to go through it, not
> without pain but without stain."
> -Anonymous

As you know, we consider blessed those who
have persevered. You have heard of Job's
perseverance and have seen what the Lord
finally brought about. The Lord is full of
compassion and mercy.
James 5:11

You cannot grasp the greatness of Job's perseverance without remembering that Job was blameless and upright from the beginning. God said so. Job was spiritually prepared for difficulty in ways that few people are. He was a righteous man.

His trials were permitted by God for the glory of God and the benefit of Job although Job knew nothing about that. Job only knew that he was the victim of this exercise and a terrible victim at that. Despite the unbearable pain of his trials Job would say, *"Though he slay me, yet will I hope in him?"* (Job 13:15). Oswald Chambers paraphrased that verse like this, *"Though He—whom you (Job's misguided friends) are misrepresenting and whom I cannot state in words—though He slay me, I will trust in the fact that He is full of the integrity I believe Him to be, and I will wait for Him."*

Job was a mature and wealthy man, well settled in an affluent life style who suddenly lost everything: barns, houses, livestock (11,500 farm animals) and servants. His entire fortune was wiped out in a single day. Every investment he owned, every bank account he had, every financial resource he possessed was destroyed in a single day; from elaborate riches to abject poverty in 24 hours. *"My hope is in Him."*

He was the proud and grateful father of ten grown children who all died together on that same awful day in a single calamity. *"My hope is in Him."*

He was the faithful husband of one wife who turned on him and on his God, telling Job he should just curse God and die. *"My hope is in Him."*

He was a robust and healthy man after years of farm work who lost his health and was reduced to sitting on an ash heap, scraping the boils that covered his body. *"My hope is in Him."*

So Job was left absolutely destitute, lonely and sick after a lifetime of hard work and success, and a lifestyle that even God agreed was blameless and upright.

And then, to turn the screws even tighter, Job was visited by three friends who spent day after day heaping on blame and bad advice. *"Though He—whom you are misrepresenting and whom I cannot state in words—though He slay me, I will trust in the fact that He is full of the integrity I believe Him to be, and I will wait for Him."*

In all of this you can find many moments when Job falters, when his perseverance jar leaks down, but you will find that aside from those moments of weakness he just perseveres. He faces God with questions, doubts, charges, and pleas but he never turns from God because through it all Job's hope is in Him. Although it is not pretty, Job perseveres. Listen to some of Job's words:

> **"Shall we accept good from God, and not trouble?" (Job 2:10).**

> **"Though he slay me, yet will I hope in him" (Job 13:15).**

> **"I know that my Redeemer lives, and that in the end he will stand upon the earth" (Job 19:25).**

In the end, when Job is bluntly confronted with the majesty and power of God, he affirms, *"I know that you can do all things; no plan of yours can be thwarted"* (Job 42:2).

Job has learned this: to the extent that we understand the power and authority of God in all things, to that extent do we know God. And to that extent we persevere. Job persevered and he did so largely because he had prepared and he fell to that level of preparation.

> "Perseverance is not a long race;
> it is many short races one after another."
> -Walter Elliot

> **Not only so, but we also rejoice in our sufferings,
> because we know that suffering produces perseverance;
> perseverance, character; and character, hope.
> Romans 5:3-5**

Or consider Gladys Aylward. She was born in 1902 to modest parents in Edmonton, London. She was an average student and became a parlor maid at the age of fourteen. At eighteen she attended a revival meeting and felt challenged to spend her life as a missionary. For eight more years she continued her work as a parlor maid, longing each day to be a missionary, until she was granted a probationary position with China Inland Mission. It was a moment of great joy for Gladys but this probationary effort ended in failure and she was not allowed to continue. She had been rejected for service in China. *"Perseverance...character... hope."*

She continued to work for another four years, always hoping for some mission opening, and at the age of 30 heard of an aging missionary woman who was looking for an assistant to carry on her work in China. Gladys accepted but did not have the funds for a steamship ticket and so she set off for Yangchuan overland with her passport, her Bible, her train tickets and 2 pounds, nine pence in funds. Her search for a mission assignment was over but her trials were to begin. *"Perseverance...character...hope."*

In Yangchuan the two women settled into a ministry to mule drivers who stayed in the town overnight. The two women would feed and house these men and tell them stories of a man named Jesus.

In short time, her mentor died and Gladys became aware of the many unwanted children in local villages. At the same time she was ministering to wounded soldiers from the Sino-Japanese war then in progress and often housed as many as 20 orphans and 40 wounded soldiers at the same time. *"Perseverance... character...hope."*

As the war intensified the number of children under her care neared 100 and she was warned to leave Yangchuan because her life was threatened. Since it was too hazardous to use the local roads she led her large brood of children 100 miles over the local mountains to a safer province. When they arrived Gladys collapsed from a combination of typhus, pneumonia, fever, malnutrition and exhaustion.

Anyone else would have returned to the safety and comfort of England but although she never fully recovered her health she continued to minister in Sian for another 10 years by sharing the gospel among the sick and helpless and in the prisons. *"Perseverance...character...hope."*

In 1947 she was forced to leave China because of the Communist Revolution. After a few years in England she returned to Taiwan and started another orphanage which she administered until her death in 1970.

Gladys Aylward had trained herself in godliness through the servant work of a parlor maid and the deliberate study of God's Word and work and much prayer.

Gladys Aylward persevered from the time of her first desire to be a missionary at the age of 18 until her death 52 years later. Gladys did not rise to the occasion; she fell to her level of preparation. *"Perseverance...character...hope."*

"There is a strength of quiet endurance as significant
of courage as the most daring feats of prowess."
-Henry Theodore Tuckernman

**I therefore, the prisoner in the Lord, beseech
you to walk worthily of the calling
wherewith ye were called.
Ephesians 4:1**

Paul encourages us (instructs us) to *"walk worthy"* of our calling. It is an instructive metaphor for our spiritual life since walking is such a lonely, measured, disciplined activity. It is a solo activity; no one can walk for you, you have to do that yourself.

It is a very mundane activity; walking draws no attention. It is a disciplined routine of keeping on in the direction of the destination. *"Walk worthy."* Good advice for perseverance.

Douglas Robert Steuart Bader was born in London in 1910 to a British army officer. As a young teen he became fascinated with airplanes and in 1928 Douglas joined the Royal Air Force as a pilot cadet. Mid-way through the two year program, Douglas' academic performance was so weak as to prompt a severe reprimand by his commanding officer. It was a wake up call for Bader and he began to study seriously. When he completed the program he was regarded as one of the best pilots in the group and, in addition, he achieved the second highest academic score, only fractions of a grade point below number one. *"Walk worthy."*

In 1931 Douglas suffered a catastrophic crash and lost both of his legs, one above the knee and one below. He spent months in recovery and was not expected to walk again since the art and science of prosthetic devices was still only one step above peg-legs. Further, no one had ever walked with two artificial limbs. It had never been done.

Bader became acquainted with a man who was designing artificial, jointed legs from aircraft aluminum, a startling development in the technology of prostheses. After months of agonizing effort, Bader became the first man in history to walk on two artificial legs. It is common today but in 1932 it was an astounding accomplishment. Further, he never used a cane. He went on to drive a car and take dancing lessons. *"Walk worthy."*

In 1932 he applied to the RAF for reinstatement but was told that he would be retired on the grounds of his disability. He then spent six years at a desk job for the Asiatic Petroleum Company.

In September 1939, immediately after the start of WWII,

Bader re-applied to the RAF and was—amazingly—accepted back for flying duties. Within six months, Bader had so proved his flying abilities with artificial legs that he was appointed squadron commander of a fighter squadron. He was not only a brilliant pilot but an astute tactician who ultimately led RAF fighter command into entirely new and far more successful tactics overall. *"Walk worthy."*

During the next 18 months Bader shot down 22 enemy airplanes making him a quadruple ace and the fifth highest scoring pilot in the RAF. Then in August 1941 he suffered a mid-air collision with a German airplane and bailed out over France where he was captured and placed in a POW camp. During the bailout he lost his legs and was again unable to walk. *"Walk worthy?"*

Bader's captors knew of his reputation and treated him with great respect. He persuaded them to allow a British plane to fly over the camp and air drop new legs. On August 19th a British bomber parachuted new legs to Douglas enabling him to walk again. In August 1942 he used those new legs to escape. *"Walk worthy."*

Douglas Bader is an inspiring example of perseverance, and his particular struggle reminds me to *"Walk worthy"* as I have need to persevere through life's difficulties.

"The repetition of small efforts will accomplish more
than the occasional use of great talents."
-Charles Spurgeon

**Therefore do not worry about tomorrow, for
tomorrow will worry about itself. Each day
has enough trouble of its own.
Matthew 6:34**

Perhaps the biggest obstacle to perseverance is looking too far into the future. We meditate on our problems, examining them for every possible consequence and forget that *"each day has enough trouble of its own."* Really, each hour, each minute has enough trouble of its own. It is good and proper to prepare for circumstances that are reasonable risks. It is wise to have a spare tire in your car and band aids in the bathroom cabinet, but despite all of our preparations we live and trust in the moment.

Perseverance is not some impressive accomplishment produced by a grand personal design. It is the simple performance of small and right behaviors in the details of life as we are burdened by difficulties and discouragements. It is most successfully accomplished by our deliberate trust in a faithful and loving God. He has promised us that He is our refuge, our savior, or comforter, our counselor, our shepherd. When we grasp that, perseverance seems more natural and possible. When we trust Him we are able to walk worthy.

"You can trust the man who died for you."
-Lettie Cowman

I lift up my eyes to the hills—
where does my help come from?
My help comes from the LORD,
the Maker of heaven and earth.
Psalm 121:1-2

Filling this jar requires constant attention. Perseverance is like walking through the dark, one step at a time until, at just the right time, in God's time, we arrive home. It is tedious but it is pleasing and honoring to God. It is a demonstration of our trust and confidence in the One who died for us, and *"without faith it is impossible to please Him"*.

Be responsible and plan for tomorrow but strive not to worry about it. There is enough to keep you occupied today. Just keep walking.

"Walk worthy" of the One who died for you.

"Though he slay me, yet will I hope in him."

"Suffering produces perseverance; perseverance, character; and character, hope."

Perseverance in. Courage for tomorrow out. Jesus always in the middle.

"One cold winter day a snail started climbing an apple tree. As he inched slowly upward, a worm stuck its head out from a crevice in the bark to offer some advice. 'You're wasting your energy. There isn't a single apple up there.' The snail kept up his slow climb. 'There will be when I get there,' he said."
-Anonymous

**Perseverance must finish its work so
that you may be mature and complete,
not lacking anything.
James 1:4**

Chapter Seven

The Patience Jar

"Patience is the ballast of the soul that
will keep it from rolling and tumbling
in the greatest storms."
-Charles Hopkins

**But thou, O man of God, flee these things;
and follow after righteousness, godliness,
faith, love, patience...
1 Timothy 6:11**

So now we move on to the patience jar. While you labor to keep that leaky perseverance jar replenished you will need to keep this one full also. No one said it would be easy. Paul described it as spiritual warfare.

Perseverance and patience are wrapped together in a very intimate way. You cannot persevere without periods of patience and you cannot maintain patience for very long without a serious commitment to persevere.

The fourth chapter of the book of Ecclesiastes talks about personal relationships and includes that descriptive statement that *"a cord of three strands cannot be easily broken."* It is generally taken to mean that a relationship of two people cannot be easily broken when they are braided together with God in the middle. In a similar way, perseverance and patience are entwined. Perseverance and patience are wound together and when you bring God into the mix so there are three strands rather than two, the connection is not easily broken.

Patience and perseverance alone are fragile, but they are durable and strong when woven together with a central strand of trust and confidence in God.

And that confidence is well grounded because the God of this universe promised that He would *"never leave you or forsake you,"* that He would be *"your shepherd,"* that He would be *"your refuge and your strength"* and you better be sure that promise jar is large enough.

"Knowing trees, I understand the meaning of patience.
"Knowing grass, I can appreciate persistence."
–Hal Borland

**And we pray this in order that you may live a life worthy of the Lord ... being strengthened with all power according to his glorious might so that you may have great endurance and patience.
Colossians 1:10-11 (abridged)**

Patience, perseverance, forbearance and persistence are so related that the original two or three Greek words used in the New Testament are translated into any and all of these English words by various translators. Linguists may criticize me for making too fine a distinction (or not enough of a distinction) but I am not dealing so much with Greek-English translation accuracy as with mental concepts that are important for our spiritual walk in times of fear, worry and anxiety.

Actually, Paul captured the idea well in Colossians 1:11 where he makes the same distinction: *"being strengthened with all power according to his glorious might so that you may have great endurance and patience."* Endurance (perseverance) and patience. They are subtly different and inextricably related and we need both.

For our purposes here let us make a distinction between perseverance which involves steadfast, active pursuit of a goal, despite difficulties or obstacles, and the passive waiting and stillness of patience with confidence in a loving and wise God..

When you struggle with fear, worry and anxiety it will be important to persevere with all the normal demands of life and with the appropriate, Godly efforts to resolve problems, while also waiting on God for the final outcome. This jar is about patience. This jar is filled with the confidence that God is at work and we can wait for Him, even as we persevere through the daily demands on our lives. *"Be still and know that I am God"* (Psalm 46:10).

"Patience is a virtue,
Possess it if you can.
Found seldom in a woman,
Never in a man."
-Unknown

But the fruit of the Spirit is love, joy, peace, patience...
Galatians 5:22

Patience is difficult because it collides with our human nature. It is simply not part of the basic human makeup to be patient. We live in a culture that does not cultivate patience. Consider the fast food industry (which you can do without actually eating it!). You watch as the vehicle in front of you stops next to a sign with pictures of food. The driver tells the sign what he wants and pulls forward. His arm reaches out with money and he pulls forward again. Then another arm from inside the building reaches out with a bag plump with food. Instant lunch!

But that's not all! We have fax messages and emails, ATMs and microwaves, digital cameras, and computers that provide information about everything imaginable at the touch of a finger. Nothing in our culture actually nurtures patience and unfortunately slowing down in traffic sends some of us into a rage. In one cartoon strip Calvin is shown holding a frozen dinner and reading the instructions. "Six minutes to cook this?" he says, "Who has time for that?"

Consider the infant, that innocent and engaging little human. When they are nice they are very nice, but when they awake in the middle of the night, hungry and wet, they do not lie in the crib and think, "Mom and Dad are pretty tired. I will just wait here and be patient until the time is more favorable for them to come and change my diaper and give me some food."

They do not think that way because they are, by their very nature, impatient. They want what they want, now. And so do we, although with age we do become far more skilled at restraining outward displays of impatience. With enough practice we can maintain a pretense of outward patience even though we are churning on the inside. Patience is unnatural, or more accurately, *supernatural.*

Patience is a fruit—a manifestation, a demonstration, a display—of the Holy Spirit living in us. It is a fruit that comes from a supernatural source. It is a resource that we can mine out of the gifts that are given to believers in Christ, but like all of those gifts it will require our participation.

> "If you are tempted to lose patience with
> your fellowman; stop and think how patient
> God has been with you."
> -Unknown

**The Lord is not slow in keeping his promise,
as some understand slowness. He is patient
with you, not wanting anyone to perish, but
everyone to come to repentance.
2 Peter 3:9**

It is helpful to grasp the grand and encouraging fact that God, Himself, is patient. It is good to remember fundamental things including how God's example of patience has affected all of our lives. He, the God of the universe who is absolute Sovereign of all things, is patient. Imagine that!

God's original plan was for man to live in a perfect relationship with Him. But sin intervened. Adam and Eve rebelled and God had no alternative but to break that relationship because He who is without sin cannot have fellowship with those who do.

What a dilemma! A perfect God and sinful people. A perfect God who loves those sinful people but who cannot have a relationship because of that sin barrier.

But God is wonderfully creative and He made a way. He knew that if there could be a perfect sacrifice for sin, there could be reconciliation. If there were someone who was able and willing to pay the penalty for sin there could be a restored relationship.

That someone was—from the very beginning—Jesus. Read Genesis 3:15 for the first hint of that plan. And as you read don't miss this simple fact: In a book that contains 1189 chapters, God's final plan for restoring His relationship with fallen man can be found in the third chapter and after that He waited! *He is patient.*

So the plan was made but God exercised patience for over a thousand chapters and for thousands of years. And then *"when the time had fully come"* (Galatians 4:4) He executed the plan. Jesus came: *"The Lamb of God who takes away the sins of the world"* (John 1:29).

He died for the sins of mankind. He suffered unspeakable physical pain but that wasn't really much compared to the spiritual agony of bearing all the sins of mankind.

No one likes to take blame when they are innocent but Jesus did just that. He took all the blame for all the sins of all time. And there had been a long wait for that to happen. So long in fact that God's original promise and plan had become blurred and forgotten so that when it happened not many people were interested. And still there are not that many interested in God's plan of redemption but through all of this, *He is patient.*

He is also patient on a personal level. He was *"patient with (me), not wanting (me) to perish"* for 33 years. He waited through my sin, my rebellious attitude, my pride, my ignorance, my resistance for 33 years. He was patient with me in a way that no human would have been patient if they could have seen my heart. He was patient as he waited for the day and the hour when I would simply surrender to His authority and acknowledge that I was without hope aside from His plan of Jesus' sacrifice. And He is still patient with me daily as I struggle and fall short of His glory. And He is patient with you. God is patient. *He is patient.*

> "Patience permits us to cling to our faith in the
> Lord when we are tossed about by suffering
> as if by surf. When the undertow grasps us we will
> realize that we are somehow being carried
> forward even as we tumble. We are actually
> being helped even as we cry for help."
> -Neal A. Maxwell

**Be patient, then, brothers, until the Lord's
coming. See how the farmer waits for the
land to yield its valuable crop and how patient
he is for the autumn and spring rains.
You too, be patient and stand firm.
James 5:7-8**

So if God is patient with us it seems fitting for us to be patient with Him. It helps to know that He has promised to constantly monitor and supervise every detail of our lives so that He is never unaware of what we are facing and the emotional baggage it creates. God knows. God cares. God is working.

God is not absent. He is not oblivious. He is not distracted. He is on the job and shaping events and circumstances for our benefit, even when it feels just the opposite. It is a useful reminder when we have need of patience. "We are actually being helped even as we cry for help."

When Elijah faced off with the prophets of Baal in a competition to see whose god would accept a burned sacrifice, he mocked those prophets by asking if, maybe, their god was in the bathroom and unavailable. Actually, that mocking had a sarcastic connection to basic pagan belief. Pagan gods were understood to have busy lives which often distracted them from attention to mortal men and women. They had romantic lives and turf wars and in-laws and other distractions so you just couldn't know when they were preoccupied.

The God and Father of our Lord Jesus Christ is not so. He is like a shepherd who constantly supervises the flock and misses even one sheep out of a hundred. (Or in our case one out of 6 billion). He is alert and knowledgeable and engaged. You can count on that and accordingly, you can have confidence in the midst of your patience.

When Israel faced off against the powerful Egyptian army, Moses could tell them, *"The LORD will fight for you; you need only to be still"* (Exodus 14:14). Be still. Be patient. More is happening than you might think.

James captured that idea in the context of a farmer waiting for his crops. *"See how the farmer waits..."* (James 5:7). It is a helpful picture. The farmer puts tiny seeds of corn into the ground and then he waits. Days pass and there is nothing visible to show for his effort although the farmer knows that much is happening below the surface. After about two weeks of typical spring weather he will see tiny shoots break the surface of the ground. If the corn stalk grows normally it will begin to form an ear in 8-10 weeks. If the plant develops as expected it will be ready for harvest in four months.

From corn seed to corn harvest requires four months of patience as the plant germinates, grows and matures. Should we be any less patient with God as He germinates, grows and matures His divine answer and guidance in the midst of fear, worry and anxiety? Apparently not since James adds, *"You too, be patient and stand firm"* (James 5:8).

Charles Spurgeon expresses James' thought like this, "Yes, the husbandman (farmer) waits. He cannot push on the months; he cannot hasten the time of the harvest home; but he does not wait in silence; in sluggishness and negligence; he keeps to his work and waits too. So do you, O Christian men! Wait for the Lord, but let it be with your lamps trimmed and your lights burning, as good servants attending to the duties of the house, until the master of the house returns to give you the reward. ...If I am a worker, I must look to God for the result, but then I must also use all the means. In fact, the Christian should work as if all depended upon him, and pray as if it all depended upon God."

"You too, be patient and stand firm"

> "Teach us, O Lord, the disciplines of patience,
> for to wait is often harder than to work."
> -Peter Marshall

A man's wisdom gives him patience.
Proverbs 19:11

Finally, it is important to know that patience is not something you are but something you do. Patience is indeed normally harder than work but it is a crucial element of fighting the spiritual battle against fear, worry and anxiety.

Scripture and history are full of those who have waited patiently for answers to their deepest desires. I love David's words in Psalm 40, *"I waited patiently for the LORD; he turned to me and heard my cry. He lifted me out of the slimy pit, out of the mud and mire; he set my feet on a rock and gave me a firm place to stand. He put a new song in my mouth, a hymn of praise to our God."* It is a beautiful list of the blessings of patience:

- Lifted out of the pits
- Feet set on a rock
- A permanent and safe place to stand
- A new song to sing.

And all of it begins with patience. *"I waited patiently for the LORD."*

William Wilberforce was a devout Christian member of Parliament in England 200 years ago. He was deeply offended by the institution of slavery because he knew that God never intended for people to own other people. Wilberforce pushed the parliament to abolish this ugly practice and nearly despaired as the years passed with no results. Surely this was a good and Godly effort. Surely God agreed that people enslaving other people was sinful. And so he spent his life writing, speaking, legislating and lobbying for the rights of slaves in England.

At one point his friend John Wesley wrote to encourage him, "If God is for you who can be against you? Be not weary of well-doing! Go on, in the name of God and the power of His might." Wesley died six days after writing that but Wilberforce persisted for 45 more years until he saw slavery abolished from England in 1833. He was a patient man.

God promised Abraham and Sarah a family and then waited until Abraham was 100 years old and Sarah something over 90 years old to deliver their first child (Genesis 15:1-5). Talk about the need for patience!

Esther survived the malicious palace intrigues of Haman who had plotted to have all the Jews in the Persian kingdom killed but then had to wait nine months to see God's final answer for the safety of her fellow Jews (Esther, chapter 7).

Missionaries who accept the challenge to translate the Bible into a primitive tongue must devote a minimum of 15-20 years just to produce the New Testament. Twenty years living in harsh conditions, far from friends and family, medical help or other comforts. Think about it: twenty years of dogged, fatiguing, hard work to produce a few hundred pages of God's Word in a language familiar to those in the area. Patience. Patience.

Patience is difficult but we are created in the image of a patient God. Since He is patient with us perhaps we can respond in kind.

Patience is not natural, it is supernatural and possible only because we have the power of God to enable us and it is an essential element in the spiritual warfare against fear, worry and anxiety.

Theodore Beza was a disciple of John Calvin who spent much of his life ministering to the Huguenots and other Protestants in France in the early days of the Reformation when there was much persecution and political resistance from the Catholic Church. There were, indeed, several small wars and massacres between the contending churches. It was a hard and dangerous time.

At one contentious moment in this period of armed conflicts between Catholics and Protestants, Beza was invited to plead the evangelical case before King Antony of Navarre. He traveled to the Castle at Nerac and pleaded the Protestant case, but although the king listened, in the end he was not sympathetic and so Beza knew that he and his protestant brothers would endure more persecution.

When the conference concluded, Beza addressed the King with these words, "From this day I am an exile from France so long as it pleases God to make His Church an anvil for the blows of His enemies. God's church is now an anvil, but remember it is an anvil which has worn out many hammers."

What a goal! To be an anvil of patience that wears out the hammers of fear and worry and anxiety because we are confident in a sustaining and purposeful God.

"We say, 'sorrow', 'disaster', 'calamity'. God says, 'chastening,' and it sounds sweet to him though it is a discord to our ears. Don't faint when you are rebuked, and don't despise the chastening of the Lord. 'In your patience possess your souls.'"
-Oswald Chambers

Therefore, as God's chosen people, holy and dearly loved, clothe yourselves with compassion, kindness, humility, gentleness and patience.
Colossians 3:12

Chapter Eight

The Praise Jar

"Praise is like a plow set to go deep into the
soil of believers' hearts. It lets the glory of
God into the details of daily living."
-C.M. Hanson

**I will praise you, O LORD, with all my heart;
I will tell of all your wonders.
Psalm 9:1**

This sixth and final jar is intended to be filled with praises
to God, praises that let the glory of God into the details of daily
living. Actually, there is no special order to these six jars, and
any of the jars can be filled in any sequence, but in the structure
of this book it is the last jar.

The metaphor of Six Stone Jars is just a figure to help you
grasp some of the spiritual weapons God has made available
to fight the battle of fear, worry and anxiety. This is not a six-
step formula for spiritual peace but a simple reminder of some
resources that God has made available to all believers. This is
not about a recipe for emotional relief but about a relationship
with the Father God who has loved you from the foundation of
the earth.

How and when you use those weapons is an individual
choice. If you find this word picture helpful, there are six jars
to fill. Try to keep them full but don't be concerned about the
sequence.

This praise jar is an easy jar to fill because there is so much material with which to fill it. Even when we cannot find the words and thoughts within ourselves to praise God who is omnipotent, omniscient, wise, loving, patient, forgiving, strong, and sovereign we can find them abundantly in Scripture, particularly in the book of Psalms. In fact, one way to praise God is to simply read the praises in Psalms back to Him. You can fill this jar to the brim with just a few well chosen, thoughtfully spoken psalms and in that sense it is an easy jar to fill.

But it is a difficult jar to fill because it is not natural to sing praises in the midst of fear and worry and anxiety. It is far more natural to express our fears or verbalize our complaints or sulk and pout than it is to praise God who is sovereign over all things, including the thing for which you are currently worried or fearful or anxious.

In order to praise God during those hard times it is important to grasp the concept. Praising God in the midst of a crisis is not expressing your appreciation for the thing that is causing anxiety: the job loss or failed relationship or financial reversal. This biblical praise is not an expression of gratitude for the fear and worry you are experiencing. It is not a Pollyanna denial of the very real troubles you are facing. It is none of that.

Praising God is an acknowledgment of His greatness and perfection, His mercy and grace and wisdom and goodness. We praise Him for His attributes and qualities before we praise Him for any particular activity in our life.

This jar is to be filled with praises for God's excellent character without which we would be hopeless. Ironically, it may include praises for the very hardship that is causing the worry because we remember that he is good in all things but it is much more than just that.

Charles Spurgeon once described our trials as, "Blessed acts of sorrow that cut a pathway to my God by chopping down the tall trees of human comfort." But Charles Spurgeon himself suffered long periods of crippling depression. He was right about the "blessed acts of sorrow" but I can only assume that his praise of God for the hardships of life was not his principle form of praise. Sometimes praise is simply an acknowledgement of God's excellence and wisdom. We should offer praise for the spiritual value of actual hardship, but it is not natural and not easy.

Actually, Scripture includes the concept of praise as a sacrifice and it is a sacrifice in two distinct ways. Praise in the midst of personal anxiety and worry is a sacrificial denial of our personal preferences for self pity and withdrawal. It is also a sacrifice of our time, energy, and thoughts to meditate upon and verbalize the excellencies of God who is, after all, thoroughly sovereign over the very issues that cause us to worry.

In the end, praises offered to God in any form are the gates by which we enter into His loving and encouraging presence.

"The climax of God's happiness is the delight
he takes in the echoes of His excellence
in the praises of His people."
-John Piper

You will call your walls 'Salvation'
and your gates 'Praise'.
Isaiah 60:18

Enter his gates with thanksgiving and
his courts with praise.
Psalm 100:4

Notice the picture that is drawn here by both the Psalmist and by Isaiah: They each have in mind the Holy city of God, surrounded by walls. Isaiah says the walls around that city will be called "salvation" because they will provide safety and security from danger in the same way that our salvation provides a wall of assurance of eternal safety and security even as we struggle with the immediate crises of life. We are not safe outside of those salvation walls. We are not safe when we linger outside of God's presence when we are distracted and consumed by our fears and worries and anxieties. We are safe only in His presence and in order to get there we must go inside the walls of our salvation and find the presence of God. We must enter that area of assurance and protection from emotional and spiritual damage.

And the way into that city, the city of safety and security … the gate by which we can find entrance… is called "Praise". Praise of God, praise to God, is like a door that we open to find His presence inside. I like that. It reminds me of something I do every day.

When I drive up to my garage I press a little button on the car's instrument panel and the garage door opens. I think the picture for us here is that when we approach the walls of God's presence the button we press to open the gate is labeled "Praise." When my spirit is downcast within me one way to penetrate the wall that seems to separate me from God is to find ways and means to praise Him. I like that. Praise Him and the gates open.

"Enter His courts with praise" (Psalm 100:4). Open the way into God's presence by offering praises to the One who loves us, saves us, cares for us, has plans for us and claims us as His own. Praise is the gate opener. Praise is the key to the reassuring presence of God. Praise allows us to penetrate the walls.

It would be easy to imagine that God is above the praises of mortal men. Why would He care if I praise Him? Would Leonardo da Vinci care if I sent him a note to tell him what good work he did in painting the Mona Lisa? Would Brett Favre care if I told him he knew how to throw a football? They would be more likely to think that I simply didn't understand what they have accomplished and that any praise I could express would have little significance because I couldn't possibly appreciate their accomplishments.

Not so with God. He loves and cherishes the praises of His children. He understands that we can't fully appreciate all that we are praising, but He loves the praises of His children anyway.

David describes God in Psalm 22 as "enthroned on the praises of Israel", or "inhabiting" the praises of Israel depending on the translator. It is a mind stretch to consider that God would even care about our praises but, clearly, He does. He likes them so much that he sits on them as if they were a cushion on His throne.

In the midst of fear and worry and anxiety, dedicate some serious time and effort to filling a jar with praise to God. Those praises will open the gates to His presence and when you look in you will find that God Himself is sitting enthroned on the very things that opened the gates. Your praises are the gate opener and God's pillow. Hard to believe, I know, but He said so.

"Come Thou fount of every blessing
Tune my heart to sing Thy praise."
-Robert Robinson

Great is the LORD, and most worthy of praise,
in the city of our God, his holy mountain.
Psalm 48:1

It is a sad thing that we should need God to tune our hearts to sing His praise, but we do. In the midst of fear and worry and anxiety our instincts are to do many things other than to praise God for His greatness and goodness. We need Him to tune our hearts like the strings of a violin to properly sing praises that are fitting. It is a good beginning to ask our God to help us as we set about to fill the praise jar. We need our hearts to be tuned. They don't sing well without it.

One big part of that tuning is to remember just why it is that we praise God. Why would we stop in the middle of a personal crisis of faith to praise God when everything is indefinite and threatening? Why would I lavish honor and admiration on God when I have no idea what He is up to and how He intends to bring this mess to a resolution?

One reason is what we just described. Praising God opens the gates to His presence. But there are several more reasons. A very good reason to do this is because He has told us to, over and over:

- *"Sing praises to the LORD"* (Psalm 9:11).
- *"Let everything that has breath praise the LORD"* (Psalm 150:6).
- *"Praise the LORD, all his works everywhere in his dominion"* (Psalm 130:322).
- *"Praise the LORD. Give thanks to the LORD, for he is good"* (Psalm 106:1).

Need more? Get a big pad of paper and search the psalms. And when that is done just keep going through all the other books and keep notes. The command is everywhere. *"Praise the Lord."*

Sometimes simple obedience is just the right thing. When Saul explained to Samuel that he saved the cattle from the Amalekites for a sacrifice to the Lord after he was told to destroy everything, Samuel answered, *"to obey is better than sacrifice"* (1 Samuel 15:22b).

On that very issue, the issue of simple obedience, God rejected Saul as King of Israel.

Now, just imagine that. God wanted Saul to destroy everything in the land of the Amalekites but Saul had another idea. He thought he would save a few animals to sacrifice in thanksgiving for the victory. Sounds good to me, but God thought otherwise. He told Saul to destroy everything and had not asked Saul for his opinion. God likes obedience more than any sacrifice we can conjure. And surely He likes our obedience of praise. *Praise the Lord.*

Another good and valid reason to praise the Lord in the depth of our anxiety is because praise changes us. It encourages us. In some mysterious way praising God enhances our affections for God like a feedback loop. Praise God and love Him more. Love Him more and praise Him more. And on and on. C.S. Lewis expressed it like this:

> "I think we delight to praise what we enjoy
> because the praise not merely expresses
> but completes the enjoyment. It is not out of
> compliment that lovers keep on telling one
> another how beautiful they are; the delight is
> incomplete until it is expressed."

Praising God completes our enjoyment of God. It completes our delight in God. Try it. *Praise the Lord.*

> "Praise God, from whom all blessings flow!
> Praise Him, all creatures here below!
> Praise Him above, ye heavenly host!
> Praise Father, Son, and Holy Ghost!"
> -Thomas Ken

Praise the LORD with the harp; make music to him on the ten-stringed lyre. Sing to him a new song; play skillfully, and shout for joy.
Psalm 33:2-3

One thing you will find if you actually think about praising God is the number of ways available to do just that. The psalmist lists harp and lyre and singing and shouts. Elsewhere the psalms talk of tambourine, dancing, cymbals, strings and flute. It is clear that God is honored by a variety of styles and methods of praise from His people. As you begin to praise, remember that you are praising God for His excellent qualities which have brought you to this place and will lead you on. You praise Him for His mercy and grace and wisdom and power and knowledge and understanding and more. Much, more. *Praise the Lord.*

All of this praise originates in the heart and will be a deliberate act of the will to express our honor for Him. It will all be a form of that interesting word, Halleluiah!

Halleluiah is actually the combined form of two Hebrew words, "halal" and "Yah". "Halal" means to celebrate something, to boast or even rave about it. "Halal" is a vigorous compliment, a resounding flattery, a clamor of admiration that actually borders on an appearance of foolishness. "Halal" is expressive and celebratory. You could "halal" your favorite athlete or rock star or politician or your fiancé.

"Yah" is an abbreviation of the Jewish holy word for God, "Yahweh". It means the same thing. It means the great and only God, the self-existent and eternal One.

Halleluiah is a one word expression of enthusiastic praise to God. It is brief but loaded with meaning. Hallelu Yah! Halleluiah! It is a great beginning, especially if you understand the original meaning. Halleluiah! *Praise the Lord.*

So what are some of the specific ways I can praise God besides the obedient sacrifice of praise in my heart and the simple exclamation of "Halleluiah"?

Well, since Jesus has told us that our mouth speaks what is in our heart, we can praise God with our lips. We can verbalize our praises. We can express aloud our affections and appreciations for God's perfect and holy character, His wisdom and love and personal interest in our pathetic little lives and problems. We can just vocally compliment God for all of His excellencies and we can do that alone in an empty room as a form of personal devotion or with and to those who are a part of our lives as a form of personal testimony, or both. *Praise the lord.*

Since God has made it clear that our bodies are temples in which His Spirit lives, we can praise Him with those temples. We can express our praises in physical ways: raised hands, bended knees and dancing feet, fasting and feasting and acts of physical service but all in the context of not offending our brothers who may have different styles of praise. *Praise the Lord.*

We can praise Him with music. We can praise Him with voice or instruments or recordings. We are blessed to live in a world suffuse with recorded music and inexpensive electronic devices on which to play it. I have a dear friend who survived a long, dark and traumatic period in his life by surrounding himself completely with God's Word and music that expressed all the dimensions of that Word. *Praise the Lord.*

Finally, we can praise Him with our lives. *"Whether you eat or drink or whatever you do, do all for the glory of God"* (1 Corinthians 10:31). I can praise Him with the simple acts of accomplishing the necessities of life in the midst of crushing heartache. I can praise Him with doing the laundry and going to work and caring for the residence He has provided. I can praise Him with the simple details of my life. *Praise the Lord.*

> "Praise God even when you don't
> understand what He is doing."
> -Henry Jacobsen

**Praise be to the God and Father of our
Lord Jesus Christ, the Father of compassion
and the God of all comfort.
2 Corinthians 1:3**

The prophet Isaiah wrote during a depressing and difficult time in Judah's history. The vicious and powerful Assyrian empire was threatening Jerusalem and there was great fear in the land. This was a time to keep those jars full because it was a time of great reason for fear and worry and anxiety. *"In the midst of all that Isaiah told the people of Judah and Jerusalem, The LORD has anointed me to ... bind up the brokenhearted, to proclaim freedom for the captives and release from darkness for the prisoners,...*[2] *to comfort all who mourn,*[3]*to bestow on them a crown of beauty instead of ashes, the oil of gladness instead of mourning, and a garment of praise instead of a spirit of despair"* (Isaiah 61:1-3).

It is a lovely reminder that God is always involved. That he is working in the midst of our darkness. That when the enemy is at the gates we can wrap ourselves in a garment of praise for His faithfulness and goodness and affection. *Praise the lord.*

"Our place and the place of the entire world system is to praise and exalt God. When people of the Bible caught a glimpse of Him, their lives were changed. Perhaps our lives remain stagnate because we do not spend enough time looking at Him."
-RogerAnderson

Praise the LORD.
Praise God in his sanctuary;
Praise him in his mighty heavens.
Praise him for his acts of power;
Praise him for his surpassing greatness.
Psalm 150:1-2

Chapter Nine

The Imperative of Trust

"All I have seen teaches me to trust the
Creator for all I have not seen."
-Ralph Waldo Emerson

Though He slay me, yet will I trust in Him.
Job 13:15

You can spend 24 hours a day frantically filling those
spiritual jars with prayer, memories of past blessings, God's
promises, and perseverance, patience and praise, but if you
undertake those efforts without conscious, personal trust in
God it is all pointless. You can keep filling those six jars but
that water of faith can only become the wine of blessing if
Jesus Christ, Himself, accomplishes the metamorphosis. And,
without faith, it is impossible to enlist His help.

Trust is the ingredient that connects us to God's help in
difficult times. The steward at the wedding in Cana could
not have filled those six stone jars without some serious trust
that the One who *"began the good work was able to carry it on to
completion"* (Philippians 1:6). And we are called to that same
level of trust.

Consider this: a man with a suitcase is standing at a bus stop.
In time the bus arrives and the man climbs aboard, and stands
near the front of the bus holding the suitcase in his arms. In fact,
he stands like that for several long miles.

After a time, one of his fellow passengers invites the man to
set his heavy burden down on the floor of the bus. He offers to
shuffle his feet aside to make room for the suitcase. But the man

resists. He clutches the suitcase to his chest and maintains his grip.

When the seated passenger offers again, the man says, "I am grateful that the bus carries my weight. I am a large man and it is very nice to be carried along like this but I don't want to burden the bus with the weight of my baggage. I am happy to carry that weight myself." Clearly the man needs a lesson in high school physics.

I suspect that God has been a frequent passenger on my bus and has seen me struggle to carry my suitcase because He offered similar good advice, *"Cast all your anxiety on him because he cares for you"* (1 Peter 5:7). In those times I have needed a Grade School lesson in spiritual physics.

"Jesus loves me! This I know,
For the Bible tells me so.
Little ones to Him belong;
They are weak, but He is strong."

There is something in our nature which makes trust difficult. We struggle to trust other people, to trust organizations and governments and it should not be surprising that we struggle to trust God. We stand with our heavy baggage because, well, because… we are strong and He just might not be strong enough.

"Life is hard.
God is good.
Don't confuse them."
-Anonymous

**In this world you will have trouble. But take heart! I have overcome the world.
John 16:33**

Life is hard. True, there are wonderful moments of peace and affection and prosperity. There are loving relationships and happy times but overall, life is hard. We make our livings by the sweat of our brow or by the strain of our eyes from our computer work. And life is hard in many other ways. Plans fail, friends leave, money goes, health declines, success fades, death takes all; sometimes tragically and suddenly.

But God is good. He rescued Israel from the cruel Pharaohs of Egypt. He brought millions of them through the dessert where they were never hungry and their clothes didn't wear out for 40 years. He delivered Daniel from a den of lions that later ate an entire banquet of people. He delivered Shadrach, Meshach and Abednego from a furnace so hot that their handlers died in the process. He sent His Son to live and die so that we could stand in the presence of God without spot or blemish. He leads us like a shepherd. He guards us like a team of Secret Service Agents. He feeds us like His sheep. God is good.

But don't confuse them. Life is not good; life is hard. It was designed by God to be hard after Adam and Eve sinned. You know that by experience every day.

God is not hard; God is good. You can see that in your own life if you will look.

Life is hard. God is good. Don't confuse them.

Life is saturated with trouble and trouble comes with his evil siblings: Fear, Worry and Anxiety. And we are prone to respond by meditating on every aspect of the trouble, looking for the hurt and disappointment that occurred in the past or might be just over the horizon.

Erwin Lutzer, pastor of Moody Church in Chicago, describes the state of the worrier as being crucified on a cross between the regrets of the past and the fears of the future. It is a brilliant analogy.

- Crucified by our own fears.

- Crucified between past regrets and future anxieties.

- Crucified by worry.

But God is good. He has promised to be our shepherd and lead us to green pastures and still waters. He is doing that. We just aren't there yet. The good Shepherd is leading and we can trust Him as we follow along through stony mountains and dessert valleys darkened by shadows of death. It is a good thing to fill those six stone jars with prayer and past blessings, God's promises and perseverance, patience and praise, but it all must be accomplished with trust or it is futile. Trust is the foundation.

Trust is what prompts you to fill these jars in the first place and trust is what sustains you in the wait between water and wine.

"When a train goes through a tunnel and it gets dark, you don't throw away the ticket and jump off. You sit still and trust the engineer." -Corrie ten Boom

You will keep in perfect peace him whose mind is steadfast, because he trusts in you. Isaiah 26:3.

We can trust God because of His very nature. He has many attributes but we must focus on these: He is good; He is wise; He is sovereign.

Think of these three attributes as forming a pyramid with "good", "wise" and "sovereign" each being one of the sides. Imagine "sovereign" as being the base of the pyramid with "good" and "wise" as the elevations. Can you picture that? If you remove one of those attributes, the pyramid could not stand. Happily for us, God is good and wise and sovereign. He is all three. He said so.

> "Christian, remember the goodness of
> God in the frost of adversity."
> -Charles Spurgeon

**Taste and see that the LORD is good; blessed is
the man who takes refuge in him.
Psalm 34:8**

God is good. The Bible is filled with references to His goodness. *"Good and upright is the Lord"* (Psalm 25:8). *"Taste and see that the Lord is good"* (Psalm 34:8). *"The Lord is good"* (Lamentations 3:25). It should be a comfort to us and a great encouragement to trust Him in the midst of fear and worry and anxiety. It should be an incentive to go about filling those six stone jars with confidence.

But true goodness is a rare thing in the affairs of men, so it is easy to be cynical and to lack a clear understanding of the very concept. So much of what we humans call goodness is tainted with self-interest and pride and other less honorable attributes. Pure goodness is an extraordinary and beautiful thing, and when it occurs, it is a glimpse of the very nature of God.

In April of 1959, I was finishing Officer Candidate School at Pensacola, FL as the prerequisite to beginning Navy pilot training. OCS was four months of fairly intense training under the discipline of Marine drill sergeants, including a demerit system that could, in the extreme, be cause for elimination.

Elimination from this pilot training program would terminate my dreams of flying since no other service would accept a failure, and civilian training was far beyond my dreams.

Flying was a long-held dream of mine so I was intensely focused on doing well and surviving the cut. I wanted to be a Navy pilot. I wanted to fly airplanes and this was my one shot.

On the day in question we were subject to a dress inspection by the Admiral. This was a critical event. Dust on the shoes, tarnish on the brass, wrinkles in the dress blues could generate enough demerits to end the dream. Fortunately, I was ready. Every element of my dress blue uniform and personal grooming was prepared and I was confident to stand before The Man for inspection.

Until we went to lunch.

The menu that noon time included some kind of sweet potato dish with a marshmallow topping. Somehow, during this frantic lunchtime I managed to spot the left side of my navy blue jacket with a small dot of that marshmallow substance. Now you might think it would be an easy thing to wipe that away with a damp cloth but there was no damp cloth, there was no time and this was some evil substance unknown outside of Navy kitchens and impervious to removal.

Worse, as I furtively worked on it with spit and handkerchief during our march to the parade grounds it took on a life of its own. It spread over my tunic until the blotch on my jacket looked like a map of Antarctica.

I was doomed. I was convinced that an infraction of this magnitude might eliminate me from pilot training.

When the inspection commenced I stood in line with my fellow classmates and waited. I had only to wait for the inevitable end and during those few minutes I planned my alternative career as a grocery bagger.

The Admiral and his team worked their way down the line, checking each candidate in turn, looking for any small infraction. The Admiral's adjutant stayed by his side to record each inspection: the name of the cadet, the infraction, and the number of demerits, "Murphy; lint on left shoulder; five demerits." "Dimatto; scuff on right shoe, ten demerits." "Smith, trousers wrinkled...etc. Anything the Admiral missed, the adjutant would point out. This was serious stuff. Your life could be forever changed.

In time I could see and hear the Admiral and his party in front of the man next to me. The Admiral was very business-like but his adjutant was in overdrive, finding and pointing out flaws that were microscopic. My end was near. It would be a relief to have this over.

When the Admiral finally stepped in front of me he visibly flinched at the map of the Antarctic on my tunic. It was so bizarre, so flagrant, and such a serious transgression that he seemed at a loss.

There was a pause of indecision during which the adjutant vigorously pointed and gestured and whispered in the Admiral's ear with a pencil eagerly poised over his clipboard. He was visibly enthralled by the prospect of prosecuting such an unprecedented offense and wanted to make sure the Admiral didn't miss any small part of the gruesome blemish. The Admiral looked and listened and considered.

And then he moved on. He just walked on by. He passed to the next man in line without comment and without assigning blame or penalty to me. The adjutant was beside himself but the Admiral cut him off with a curt gesture and moved on.

It was over. I had been spared by one man's moment of goodness. I had been delivered from my worst fears by the undeserved and thoroughly unexpected mercy of a considerate man. It was a rare thing. It was a lesson in grace. It is now 50 years later and I have never forgotten.

It reminds me of my sin. Why would a holy, righteous God see the contamination of my sin and yet make a way for me to be spared? Why would he look at those blemishes, while a vocal and articulate accuser pointed out every detail, and still find a way to accept me into His kingdom? Why? Because He is good in addition to being wise and sovereign. And that goodness gives me confidence to trust Him.

"We walk the bridge of life. Can we not trust its safety on the two great resting-places of God's wisdom?"
-Phillips Brookes

**Oh, the depth of the riches of the wisdom
and knowledge of God!
Romans 11:33**

God is good and wise and sovereign. He is all three. The pyramid is solid and stable. His goodness is enchanting and His sovereignty is crucial but without confidence in His infinite wisdom how could we trust?

Wisdom is a wonderful thing and we see it, however dimly, in many of the technical marvels that man has wrought. There is impressive worldly wisdom involved in the design of buildings and ships and railroads. If not, how could we trust them? If we did not trust the wisdom of brilliant engineers and craftsmen, how could we ever board an airliner or cruise ship? Ride an elevator? Trust ourselves to drive the interstate at 70 miles per hour? How could we entrust private and personal data to a computer?

When my son Victor was five, he went home with my sister and her husband for a couple of weeks in Ohio. On the way back to our home in Connecticut their route passed over the Bear Mountain Bridge which spans the Hudson River 50 miles north of New York City. This is an impressive structure of almost one half mile in length, crossing the river 135 feet in the air. The two support towers are 351 feet high and can be seen from a great distance as you approach the bridge. It is a striking view as the bridge comes into view with that ribbon of concrete and steel crossing thousands of feet of open water at a great height and suspended only by slender cables.

Certainly Victor was impressed. His five-year-old mind quickly focused on the issues involved in trusting his life to that bridge and he began to mutter his boyish observations. "Oooh, that's a big bridge!" "That bridge is real high!" "That water looks deep!" His mind was fully engaged in the issue of trust.

As they passed the on-ramp Victor grew silent and just watched with wide, little-boy eyes as the car traveled the half mile of bridge span high above the swirling Hudson River. Once across, when the car had resumed its travel on hard ground, Victor sat up, looked back at the Bear Mountain Bridge and announced with a smile and a loud voice, "Who's afraid of big bridges?"

"Who's afraid of big bridges?" Only those who don't understand and trust the people who had the technical wisdom to create and maintain the big bridges.

"Who's afraid of the future?" Only those who don't understand and trust the One who has all wisdom and who holds the future in His hands with all the power of a sovereign God. *"When I am afraid, I will trust in you"* (Psalm 56:3).

"We cannot but admit that not even the
least thing takes place unless it is ordered by
God. For who has ever been so concerned
and curious as to find out how much hair
he has on his head? There is no one. God,
however, knows the number. Indeed, nothing
is too small in us or in any other creature, not
to be ordered by the all-knowing and all-
powerful providence of God."
-Huldrych Zwingli

The LORD does whatever pleases him,
in the heavens and on the earth,
in the seas and all their depths.
Psalm 135:6

God is sovereign and He is supreme. He is self-governing. He has no higher authority. God is completely independent and in charge of all things. John Piper refers to this as "the God-centeredness of God."

It sounds strange to our ears as if it is arrogant or insensitive, but when it pertains to God it is fully appropriate. How could He not be "God-centered" if He is the source of all power and wisdom and goodness? In that case I want Him to be God-centered because that is my only hope. Think about it.

God is sovereign. He controls every detail of my life and has His own perfect plan for every circumstance, all designed to bring me safely home. It is difficult to grasp and even more difficult to trust, and yet if we can allow human devices to have sovereign authority over critical aspects of our lives why do we struggle with the sovereignty of God? Consider this...

All modern airliners are equipped with elaborate electro-mechanical systems that allow them to land automatically. When the weather completely obscures visual reference to the airport, these systems can be engaged by the pilot to fly the airplane for the final several miles to a landing on the airport. In the cockpit it is a surreal experience to engage the autopilot and simply watch as the automated systems control the speed and altitude and course of the airplane along a precise glide path to the selected runway to bring the airplane home.

During this time the throttles travel back and forth as necessary to adjust power and speed, the controls move as if responding to an invisible hand and the airplane turns and pitches to remain on course and altitude. All during this procedure, electronic voices and warning lights inform the crew of significant events.

At the critical moment of touchdown, the throttles move back, the airplane's nose lifts gently and the wings level to allow the landing gear to meet the earth in a gentle landing. Immediately after that touchdown, the brakes are automatically applied and the ground steering engages to slow the airplane and maintain a perfectly straight course along the runway centerline until the airplane is brought to a full stop. It is all done with incredible precision and finesse, almost always far beyond the capabilities of any human pilot.

The process is made possible by using three independent autopilot computers all working at the same time and all sharing data with each other. If any one autopilot exceeds some specified limitation, it is immediately voted out of the loop and the other two continue the approach as if nothing happened. These autopilots send signals to hydraulic controls that constantly adjust the airplane's path. It is a synchronized event with continuous feedback to cockpit instruments to tell the pilots just how the landing approach is proceeding. During this maneuver the autopilot has sovereign control of the airplane. It can turn and bank and climb and dive and change speed as it wills for the desired purpose of bringing us home. In a technical sort of way it is sovereign, and the safety of all on board is dependent on that sovereignty.

The total system that allows an automated landing processes more data than any human brain could handle. In this limited instance it knows more and can do more than any mortal. GPS receivers and gyros and accelerometers and electronic ground signals and computers (and much more) all process streams of data and interact in ways that exceed human capability but require extreme trust on the part of the flight crew. Accordingly, for a pilot, the process of flying an automated approach to landing is not difficult but it does demand significant trust in a very smart system that actually knows more than the pilots about this particular procedure, and can do more than the pilots in this situation to bring them all safely home.

Sound a little like God's Sovereignty? Certainly it is a flawed analogy on many levels, but it is a glimpse into our challenge of placing serious trust in the One who knows everything and can do everything and whose plan and purpose is to bring us safely home.

There is far more going on behind the scenes of our lives than we could ever know or process, but the One who is sovereign is able and willing to evaluate it all, take perfect, decisive action and guide us safely home. He is sovereign.

> "The only rest there is, is in abandonment to the love of God. There is security from yesterday-
> 'You have hedged me behind'; security for tomorrow- 'and before'; and security for today, 'and laid your hand upon me.'"
> -Oswald Chambers

**Trust in the LORD with all your heart and lean not
on your own understandings, in all your ways
acknowledge him, and he will make your paths straight.
Proverbs 3:5-6**

There is much in life that demands analysis and decision making. In many circumstances, God has imparted to us all of the knowledge and wisdom necessary to move forward. We do not need direct divine intercession to clean the garage or to make the morning coffee. There is much that God has given to our discretion and talents.

In the midst of fear and worry and anxiety we often encounter circumstances that simply have no apparent, immediate resolution. We do not know what to do and we are forced to *"be still and know that He is God"*

Chuck Swindoll has beautifully paraphrased that classic Bible passage from Proverbs 3 like this,

"Throw yourself completely upon the Lord – that is cast all your present and future needs on Him who is your intimate Savior-God… finding in Him your security and safety.

Do this with all your mind and feelings and will.

In order to make this possible, you must refuse to support yourself on the crutch of human ingenuity.

Instead, recognize His presence and concern in each one of your circumstances.

Then He (having taken full control of the situation) will smooth out and make straight your paths, removing each obstacle along the way."

In the midst of uncertainty, fear, worry, and anxiety, it is natural for us to seek out answers based on our personal knowledge even when it is clear that there is little for us to do but trust God who is good and wise and sovereign. It is natural for us to support ourselves on the crutch of human ingenuity. And those are the very times when we need the resources of our six stone jars. Six empty jars that can be filled with prayer, memories of past blessings, God's promises and our perseverance, patience and praise. And all of that can only be done as we trust the One who is good and wise and sovereign and who is always working to bring us safely home.

"Trust in yourself and you are doomed to disappointment; trust in your friends and they will die and leave you; trust in money and you may have it taken from you; trust in reputation and some slanderous tongue may blast it; but trust in God, and you are never to be confounded in time or eternity."
-Dwight L. Moody

I know him whom I have believed, and I am persuaded that he is able to guard that which I have committed unto him against that day.
2 Timothy 1:12

Chapter Ten

Six Jars Full

"Worry does not empty tomorrow of its sorrow;
it empties today of its strength."
-Corrie Ten Boom

**Therefore do not worry about tomorrow, for
tomorrow will worry about itself. Each day has
enough trouble of its own.
Matthew 6:34**

Some years ago there was a TV commercial which showed an attractive and sympathetic looking young woman in what appeared to be a medical office. This gentle lady looked directly into the TV camera with compassionate eyes and asked all of those who were watching, "Do you worry? Are you ever anxious?" She then went on to say with an expression of affectionate concern, "If so, you could have 'Generalized Anxiety Disorder'". Then she went on to pitch the benefits of the medication that sponsored the ad.

When I look at the internet and Google the definition of that "Generalized Anxiety Disorder" it is described as, "a pattern of frequent, constant worry and anxiety over many different activities and events."

While I do not understand the complexities of psychiatric evaluation, I am convinced that a significant percentage of the world's population suffers from "frequent worry and anxiety over different activities and events." In fact, if you do not have routine, recurring anxiety you might need some other medication to enhance your awareness of reality because life is riddled with difficulties, uncertainties, troubles and adversity.

Fear and worry and anxiety are the natural, human response to all of those hardships and are woven into the fabric of our lives like a virus. Worry is a part of being human. In the Garden of Gethsemane Jesus was so anxious that He sweat blood.

Do you worry? Are you ever anxious? I certainly hope so because the only alternative would appear to be life in a coma. The question is not if you worry but what resources you have to cope with the worry when it comes. The world has many remedies for fear, worry and anxiety but most do not attack the root problem. One advertisement that headlines PEACE OF MIND is a commercial for motor oil. One that promotes WORRY FREE LIVING is an ad for rental furniture.

In addition to the frivolous, there are countless promotions for herbal remedies, meditation, vacation resorts, aroma-therapy candles and an entire pharmacology of herbal extracts and psychotropic medications. If you Google "peace of mind" you will find nearly 40 million references. Clearly there is a longing for freedom from the heartache and misery of fear and worry and anxiety.

"Worry is interest paid on trouble before it is due."
-William Ralph Inge

**Who of you by worrying can add a
single hour to his life?
Matthew 6:27**

The long term remedy for fear, worry and anxiety is not found in candles or mantras or pharmacology. Neither is it some secret ritual or religious formula. There is no mysterious recipe or procedure that drains away the ache.

The treatment for these maladies is a relationship with God through His son, Jesus Christ. Fear and worry and anxiety are disarmed in the presence of God. *"There is no fear in love. But perfect love drives out fear"* (1 John 4:18).

Think of that! Fear itself becomes afraid in the presence of God. Worry gets very nervous when God is brought into the picture. Anxiety is frightened when we appeal to God. Isn't that a nice thought? Fear and worry and anxiety are no better than schoolyard bullies and they are intimidated by any attempt to strengthen our relationship with God who is good and wise and sovereign. And that relationship can be cultivated and developed with the many spiritual tools described in the Bible.

We have considered some of those spiritual weapons by using the metaphor of Six Stone Jars described in this book. It is not some secret religious rite but a picture of how we can draw closer to God in the midst of great difficulty. It is not about a recipe or a ritual but a relationship.

At the wedding at Cana, the steward faced personal ruin by underestimating the crowd's appetite for wine, and he found deliverance from that terrifying moment by following the directions of a young carpenter who offered some illogical advice: *"fill those jars with water."*

Imagine the skepticism of the steward. He didn't need more water, he needed wine. No rational person would think that water could be transformed into wine by sitting in a stone jar. The whole idea was preposterous.

But the steward really had no other option so he ordered the jars to be filled with water and when he tasted the contents it was not only wine, but it was the best wine of the day! The steward's trust was well placed because the One who had promised was willing and able.

Water into wine with Jesus as the agent of change. He is willing. He is able.

"Worriers spend a lot of time shoveling smoke."
-Claude McDonald

I have told you these things, so that in me you may have peace. In this world you will have trouble. But take heart! I have overcome the world.
John 16:33

In the midst of fear and worry and anxiety you can think of your spiritual resources as being six ingredients with which to fill six stone jars that stand empty. You can imagine yourself as a steward who has run out of wine and who is instructed to fill the jars and trust the one who gave that instruction for the end result. You can fill these jars in faith and then just wait on the One who is good and wise and sovereign.

Prayer

"Whether we like it or not, asking is the rule of the Kingdom. If you may have everything by asking in His Name, and nothing without asking, I beg you to see how absolutely vital prayer is."
–Charles Spurgeon

Do not be anxious about anything, but in everything, by prayer and petition, with thanksgiving, present your requests to God.
Philippians 4:6

Imagine an empty stone jar and fill it with personal, diligent prayer regarding the very things that are causing your stress. It is not stupid. It is God's idea. Fill it up.

Remember the Blessings of the Past

"The richness of life lies in memories we have forgotten."
–Cesare Pavese

**I will remember the deeds of the LORD;
yes, I will remember your miracles of long ago.
Psalm 77**

There is much we have forgotten about the goodness and favor of God. We all have a history of blessings large and small that when remembered are a source of encouragement that God is able and willing and caring. In that there is hope. Fill another jar with this resource.

Remember God's Promises

He has promised much. He has promised to be our Comforter, our Refuge, our Strength, our Protector, the Lover of our soul, our Shepherd, our Rescuer and our Hope. All of these are sprinkled through the pages of Scripture with examples and descriptions. Just consider Paul's take on this one. *"For no matter how many promises God has made, they are 'Yes' in Christ."*

Pour these into an empty jar and wait for The Lamb of God to make a difference.

Perseverance

"Great works are performed not by
strength but by perseverance."
– Samuel Johnson

**Blessed is the man who perseveres under trial,
because when he has stood the test,
he will receive the crown of life that God
has promised to those who love him.
James 1:12**

Both Paul and James make the link between difficulties and the development of perseverance. It is not a natural trait for any one to think they can benefit from suffering, but it can be done. Both of these New Testament writers also agree that perseverance produces character and maturity.

The writer of Hebrews reminds us that we have a great audience in heaven and for that reason alone we should *"throw off everything that hinders and the sin that so easily entangles, and run with perseverance the race marked out for us"* (Hebrews 12:1).

This persistence is not stubbornness or obstinacy. It is not headstrong, inflexible behavior. This persistence is the constant fulfillment of routine personal and spiritual responsibilities in the midst of troubles that cause fear and worry and anxiety. It requires constant, diligent self-discipline while relying on the comfort and assistance of the Holy Spirit.

Remember that this is a leaky jar and will require constant attention. Fill it up. Keep on filling.

Patience

> "There are times when God asks nothing of his children except silence, patience and tears."
> -C. S. Robinson

Be still and know that I am God.
Psalm 40:10

For those who believe that Jesus Christ is their Savior and Lord, and their bodies are the temple of the Holy Spirit, patience is one of the fruits. It is not that we are suddenly endowed with some spiritual Prozac that generates a spirit of serenity. It is that we are empowered with the new and strange ability to wait for God because we know He is. It is a fruit that must be cultivated, but it is a fruit. It grows in the life of the Christian who nurtures it because the seed has been planted as one dimension of this new life.

Patience is difficult precisely because it requires us to do nothing. At least seven times in Scripture there is that command to *"Be still…"* The Hebrew words mean to "rest", "be quiet", "wait", "be silent".

But think: Is God in control? Does He have a plan? Has He promised to lead? What if He is good and wise and sovereign…?

Then there can be patience.

Rest. Wait. Be quiet.

Patience is a strange jar. You fill this one by doing nothing. Imagine that.

Praise

"Praise now is one of the great duties of the redeemed.
It will be their employment forever."
-Albert Barnes

Praise the Lord. Praise God in His sanctuary;
praise Him in His mighty heavens.
Psalm 150:1

In the midst of fear and worry and anxiety it is not natural to pause and sing praises to God.

But, Peter said it like this, *"Praise be to the God and Father of our Lord Jesus Christ! In his great mercy he has given us new birth into a living hope through the resurrection of Jesus Christ from the dead"* (1 Peter 1:3).

We don't praise God for the nasty circumstances nor do we praise Him because we expect something in return. We praise God because of who He is, what He has already done and what he has promised us in eternity.

Praise opens the gates to God's presence in ways that are truly peculiar. There is some unexplained spiritual force that opens the doors to God's presence when we pause to consciously praise Him. When we shift our focus from our immediate problems and our personal pain to the majesty and greatness of God, the gates swing wide to a fresh vision of the One who has loved us from the foundation of the earth.

Fill it up. Fill it with the simple praises of a child who admires his Father even when that child is unsure of what the Father is doing at the moment. Fill it up and wait for the wine.

"Human life, old and young, takes place
between hope and remembrance."
-Franz Grillparzer

My comfort in my suffering is this:
Your promise preserves my life.
Psalm 119:50

In the middle of fear, worry and anxiety God has given us multiple spiritual resources. One way to remember six of those resources is to imagine them as resources with which to fill six stone jars and wait for God's mighty hand to convert them to wine. Fill these jars with prayer, memories of past blessings, God's promises, perseverance, patience and praise.

John Bunyan's classic book, PILGRIMS PROGRESS is an analogy of the Christian life. It tells the story of a man who discovers the Gospel and sets out from his hometown "The City of Destruction" (this sinful world environment) and becomes a pilgrim wanderer on his way to "The Celestial City" (Heaven).

The central character is a man named Christian who has multiple adventures which are all little pictures of what believers experience as they seek to follow Christ. The book is so powerful and enlightening that 200 year ago, many pastors owned only two books: the Bible and Pilgrim's Progress. It is a wonderful book. It is as fresh and meaningful in the 21st Century as it was when it was published in 1678. Read it in a modern translation. Read it in a child's version to your children. Get the video. Listen to the recording. It is immensely instructive.

At one point in the book, Bunyan describes our human struggle with fear, worry and anxiety in a vivid way. He tells a story of Christian and his traveling companion "Hopeful" who stray from the path (sound familiar?) and are captured by the Giant Despair who lives in Doubting Castle. Don't miss the analogy.

The Giant throws them into a stinking dungeon under Doubting Castle and beats them periodically until they are near to giving up hope. It is a vivid picture of anyone caught up in the misery of fear and worry and anxiety; captured in doubt and stuck in a cell with regular emotional beatings. That's what fear and worry do. They reside in doubt, they are ruled by despair and they constantly punish and abuse. They love doing that. Fear and worry grow into giants who cruelly abuse us and steal our hope.

So Christian and Hopeful are in the worst possible state of discouragement and the giant's wife suggests he counsel the prisoners to kill themselves. After all, they are not only in this deplorable condition but they are at least partly responsible for being there by leaving the right path.

The next morning the giant visits them and recommends suicide, "Why should you choose life since it is filled with such bitterness?" Then the giant moved to beat them again but he fell into a fit because sunlight began streaming in through cracks in the wall. Did you get that? Doubt and fear and hopelessness thrive in darkness; darkness of soul, darkness of spirit and darkness of the body. The giant can only function well in spiritual darkness. Despair falls ill in the presence of the light of truth.

When the giant leaves, Hopeful encourages Christian to see that suicide is deeply offensive to God and should not ever be an option. Following that there is an interesting short passage in which Hopeful encourages Christian

- To pray
- To remember past blessings
- To persevere
- To be patient

With these jars full, Christian woke up the next morning with these words, "What a fool I am to lie in a stinking dungeon when I can freely walk away. I have a key in my bosom called *Promise* that will open any door in Doubting Castle."

Now, with five jars full, they open the door to the dungeon, then the door to the courtyard and finally the gate to the castle. The giant briefly pursues them but cannot function in the light of day and so they escape and return to the right path with *Praises*.

Six jars full and delivered from the dungeon of Doubting Castle and the Giant Despair. If it worked 350 years ago it will work today because God has not changed.

> "The branch of the vine does not worry, and toil, and rush here to seek for sunshine, and there to find rain. No; it rests in union and communion with the vine; and at the right time, and in the right way, is the right fruit found on it. Let us so abide in the Lord Jesus."
> -Hudson Taylor

**Jesus said to the servants "Fill the jars with
water"; so they filled them to the brim. Then
he told them, "Now draw some out and take
it to the master of the banquet." They did so,
and the master of the banquet tasted the water
that had been turned into wine.
John 2:7-9**

Trouble happens. It is a certainty. Trouble happens to everyone.

Trouble never comes alone. It always brings its evil twin of Fear and Worry and Anxiety.

God has purposes for the troubles we experience; He wants us to mature in character and perseverance with hope, and that can only happen as we work through the painful emotional responses to our troubles with the right weapons.

God did not give us a silver bullet for erasing worry, and there is no medication that succeeds in doing anything more than masking the real issues. Trouble and its evil twins must be battled with the spiritual tools that God has carefully crafted for our use.

When life presses in with fear and worry and anxiety, you can fight that conflict with six spiritual weapons that can be remembered as the material with which to fill six stone jars.

Fill a jar with *prayer*
Fill a jar with all the ways that God has blessed you and delivered you in the *past*.
Fill a jar with God's *promises*
Fill a jar with *perseverance*
Fill a jar with *patience*
Fill a jar with *praises* of the God who cares for you.

In all of this remember that you are not working on a formula but on a relationship with God. And that relationship is one you can lean on. He said so.

"LEAN HARD"
-Anonymous

Child of My love, lean hard.
And let Me feel the pressure of thy care;
I know thy burden child, I shaped it;
Poised it in Mine own hand; made no proportion
In its weight to thy unaided strength.
For even as I laid it on, I said,
"I shall be near and while she leans on Me,
This burden shall be mine, not hers;
So shall I keep My child within the circling arms
Of My own love." Here lay it down, nor fear
To impose it on a shoulder which upholds
The government of the worlds
Yet closer come;
Thou art not near enough.
I would embrace thy care;
So I might feel My child reposing on My breast.
Thou lovest Me? I knew it. Doubt not then;
But, loving me, lean hard.

About the Author

Dan Manningham has been married to his wife Fran for 50 years. They have 7 children and 28 grandchildren. They are both NANC Certified Biblical Counselors with an active counseling ministry within their church. He is a preaching elder in their local church and occasional speaker at other churches and conferences.

They have served as short term missionaries and/or visited mission fields in Mali (West Africa), Kenya, Tanzania, Papua, Papua New Guinea, Costa Rica and Brazil and countries in Central Asia.

Dan has served on the Board of Directors at Mission Aviation Fellowship, Mission Safety International, PACTEC, Mansfield Christian School and Richland Pregnancy Services. He is retired after 33 years at United Airlines where his last position was 747 Captain.

Dan has published several hundred articles and three books on aviation safety issues but this is his first effort at Christian writing. He can be contacted by email at stonejars@yahoo.com, or visit his Blogspot: http://stonebooks.blogspot.com

Six Stone Jars